The Book of the BR Standard Class 5 4-6-0s

By
Ian Sixsmith

Richard Derry

Proudly ensconced in the roundhouse at Willesden, 26 May 1954. It would afterwards move on to Bath Green Park, then part of the Southern Region. A.R. Carpenter, www.transporttreasury.co.uk

Irwell Press Ltd.

Copyright IRWELL PRESS LIMITED

ISBN 978-1-906919-32-0

**For Ian Temple, enthusiast and
admirer of the BR Class 5s**

First published in the United Kingdom in 2011
by Irwell Press Limited, 59A, High Street, Clophill,
Bedfordshire MK45 4BE
Printed by Short Run Press Ltd., Exeter

Contents

A New Black Five	Page 5
A Mixed Reception?	Page 31
Concerning Tables	Page 39
The Record	Page 40

Acknowledgements

Most grateful thanks for guidance in the compilation of this 'Book Of' are due to Allan C. Baker, Eric Youldon, Andrew Sumpter, the Transport Treasury, Peter Kemmett, Brian Penney, Peter Groom, Colin Stacey of Initial Photographics, Chris Hawkins, George Reeve and Hamish Stevenson. There is still every likelihood of error of course (engine picking is like that) and these are the authors' alone.

The BR Standard Class 5 4-6-0 in as original condition as it is possible to be, other than the works grey with which it ran its first few miles. It had been ex-works in grey for its trials on 11 April 1951 and was back in after a few days to be painted and fully lined out by 20 April. Original 'panelling' on the valence of the running plate rather than a line at the lower edge. It is at Neasden shed on 25 April 1951, the day before its presentation to the British Transport Executive big-wigs at Marylebone. The evening of the exhibition it worked a Cricklewood-Derby freight and within days was observed at Manchester Central, then Sheffield and Crewe.

A New Black Five

Nearly a Pacific

There is not a lengthy developmental story to the BR Class 5 4-6-0s. Designed at Doncaster, they were a variation, a development, of a type long in use and thoroughly proven. Hundreds of examples of the Stanier LMS 'Black Five' predecessor design had been operating since the 1930s; indeed it could be argued that the 4-6-0 wheel arrangement was if not obsolescent, then approaching that condition; a landmark in the development of the steam locomotive it wasn't.

Earlier volumes in the 'Book of' series dealt with BR Standards at either end of the order of things, the Class 7 Britannia Pacifics and the 9F 2-10-0s. These by contrast both involved much developmental work; they were entirely new designs and were arrived at in their final form only after various proposals came and went. Six months after the formation of British Railways, four Pacific types were envisaged – express and mixed traffic and class 8 (later upgraded to 9) 2-8-2. What emerged of course was quite a bit different. The new BR Class 5 would have been one of the Pacifics and again an entirely new design. There was no Class 5 4-6-0 envisaged at first but the Class 5 4-6-2 became, as E.S. Cox writes (*British Railways Standard Steam Locomotives*, Ian Allan, 1966) 'the subject of particular heart searching' because it was seen as a borderline case.

If there was one type the new BR was generously endowed with it was the mixed traffic outside cylinder 4-6-0; moreover they all weighed a fair bit less than the putative Pacific and the widest possible line availability was desired.

What happened was that the various costs/advantages of the Class 5 4-6-2 over a 4-6-0 were duly assessed with as strict an eye as possible. A Pacific, with its wide firebox, would be more efficient (i.e. with low combustion rates) on the day to day average of 4-6-0 working throughout the country, thus representing a saving in coal. Yet a 4-6-2 would cost more than a 4-6-0 and it would always have the extra cost of the maintenance of the trailing truck. Moreover the turntables at many places, while too small for a Pacific, would happily turn a 4-6-0. Now, as Cox relates, the idea was desirable that the Class 5 4-6-2 should have some extra capacity above the existing Black Fives, B1s and Halls and the rest so it was determined to have the Class 6 4-6-2 instead of a Class 6 and a Class 5 4-6-2. The Class 5 would then be just that, effectively a Black Five/B1/Hall; its cylinders and valve gear would be like that of the Pacifics – the wheels at 6ft 2in would be identical (and larger than the 6ft of the Black Five) but the boiler would be the very design of Stanier, of 1934, as honed by Ivatt. So our BR Class 5 evolved in the minds of Riddles, Bond and the others and on the drawing board from an entirely new design of Pacific to an existing design modified only in detail.

The boiler used in the BR Class 5 was that arrived at by Ivatt in the 44800 series built from 1944. The BR version kept the boiler pressure, 225lb/sq.in.; it was the range of fittings which made it look so different. The idea had been to have a double chimney, but the contemporary work at Swindon on optimising chimney and blastpipe diameter meant the designers felt confident that the locomotive draughting would be good across the range of duties likely to be encountered if a correctly proportioned single chimney was used. Cox wrote that they were content to leave any double chimney, multiple blastpipe developments to the future.

The first the outside world knew of the construction of the BR Class 5s was the announcement in early 1950 of thirty in the following (1951) Building Programme. The building of pre-Nationalisation types had now largely ended; a number of Ivatt Class 4 2-6-0s were still to appear after the emergence of 73000 and B1s continued to be built for a further twelve months. Of 400 Standards to be built in 1951, thirty would be Class 5 4-6-0s, 73000-73004 for the Scottish Region and 73005-73039 for the London Midland, all built at Derby. It would be some years before any were

73001 brand new and already the alterations have begun – different lining for instance on the running plate valence. Covers still over the lubricators.

A few weeks after 73000, 73001 was also at Marylebone, on 23 May 1951, in company with brand new 75000 (behind) and 70009 ALFRED THE GREAT (in front). The diesel 10100 was also there along with four standard wagons and four standard coaches.

built at Doncaster, the home, as it were, of the design.

73000 duly appeared on exhibition at Marylebone station (convenient for the senior Officers at the adjacent 'Kremlin' HQ of the Railway Executive) on 26 April 1951 and afterwards worked an evening goods from Cricklewood yard back to Derby, which was to be its home. It was followed into service that year by a further twenty-eight, 73001-73028, but 1952 saw only one finished, 73029, completing works order No.5122 at Derby in the January. 73030 was not built until June 1953, again at Derby, the first of works order No.6230. The rest followed as in the table. From April 1951 to June 1957 was the time it took to complete the building of the class and during that period the cost of construction, not surprisingly, went up. While 73000 and its tender had cost £17,603, 73171 ran out at no less than £27,000.

The boiler carried by the Class 5 was designated Standard No.3 and was of course more or less identical to its Black Five predecessor, or at least that fitted to 45472 onwards. The only difference was a slight increase in the heating surface of the superheater. Crewe supplied 140 boilers, ten of which were spare; Doncaster built ten and the remaining 34, of which two were spare, were constructed at Darlington. So it was that Derby built no boilers at all despite its lions share of the BR Class 5s. In fact the LMS had concentrated all boiler construction at Crewe long before; Derby had indeed not built any after about 1926. Boiler numbers were: 836-865, 965-966, 993-1012, 1168-1192, 1367, 1492-1506, 1606, 1609-1643, 1750-1796, 1871, 1897-1898, 1905-1906, 1909-1911; total 184.

BUILDING AND BASIC DETAILS (After Talbot#)

Nos.	Annual Programme	Built at	Building Dates	Tender Type	Tender Nos.
73000-73004	1951	Derby	4/51-6/51	1	794-798
73005-73009	1951	Derby	6/51-7/51	1	799-803
73010-73029	1951	Derby	9/51-1/52	1	804-823
73030-73039	1952	Derby	6/53-9/53	1	864-873
73040-73049	1952	Derby	10/53-12/53	1	874-883
73050-73052	1953	Derby-	4/54-5/54	1G	989-991
73053-73054	1953	Derby	6/54	1H	992-993
73055-73064	1953	Derby	6/54-10/54	1H	994-1003
73065-73074	1953	Derby	10/54-12/54	1C	1004-1013
73075-73079	1954	Derby	4/55-5/55	1C	1014-1018
73080-73089	1954	Derby	6/55-9/55	1B	1206-1215
73090-73099	1955	Derby	10/55-12/55	1C	1272-1281
73100-73109	1955	Doncaster	8/55-1/56	1B	1282-1291
73110-73119	1955	Doncaster	10/55-12/55	1F	1292-1301
73120-73124	1955	Doncaster	1/56-2/56	1B	1302-1306
73125-73134*	1956	Derby	7/56-10/56	1B	1413-1422
73135-73144*	1956	Derby	10/56-12/56	1C	1423-1432
73145-73154*	1956	Derby	1/57-6/57	1B	1433-1442
73155-73159	1956	Doncaster	12/56-1/57	1B	1443-1447
73160-73171	1956	Doncaster	1/57-5/57	1B	1448-1459

BR1: inset, 7 tons, 4,250 gallons, no fall plate.
BR1B: flush sided, 7 tons, 4,725 gallons, fall plate.
BR 1C: flush sided, 9 tons, 4,725 gallons, fall plate.
BR 1F: flush sided, 7 tons, 5,625 gallons, fall plate.
BR1G: inset, 7 tons, 5,000 gallons, fall plate.
BR1H: inset, 7 tons, 4,250gallons, fall plate.
Southern Region tenders did not have water pick-up apparatus.

#E. Talbot, *A Pictorial Record of BR Standard Steam Locomotives*, OPC, 1982
*British-Caprotti valve gear.
Total 172

Inside Derby works, 11 June 1951; 73005 nearing completion (its frames had been laid by 20 May) and 73006 with boiler on; tenders to right and frames and cylinders of what will probably become 73007 on left. M.N. Bland, www.transporttreasury.co.uk

More exhibitions. Eastbourne goods yard on 2 June 1951. Our 73001 (nearest) had worked down light from Derby; the other two Standards were 75000 and 70009 again, its companions from Marylebone of a week before; 75000 by now was working from Swindon shed and the Britannia was at Nine Elms, on temporary secondment to the Southern as it were. The diesel 10100 was there too, and was hauled back to Derby by 73001 at the close of the exhibition.

73050 complete and in grey at Derby works paint shop, 29 April 1954. At the time 73051 was almost complete in the erecting shop, 73052 had its boiler mounted, 73053 was at the level of frames and cylinders while the frames only existed of 73054 and 73055. 73050 would later go south for display at the International Railway Congress exhibition at Willesden roundhouse, travelling with new Derby diesel shunter 13046, which is almost certainly the one behind. Eric Blakey, www.transporttreasury.co.uk

73050 on its way south in a train with 13046, trundles (connecting rods removed) past the Casserley family home at Berkhamsted on 17 May 1954. H.C. Casserley, courtesy R.M. Casserley.

A new Caprotti Class 5 at Derby works, 18 November 1956, 73138 destined for Holyhead. As outlined in the text, the Caprottis were perhaps not as concentrated as they might have been; by this time the allotment of engines to Regions was progressing to 'a plan' according to the need for Class 5 power and altering it to concentrate the Caprottis was presumably not seen as worthwhile.

Caprotti Valve Gear

The BR Class 5s were perhaps most notable for the application of the distinctive 'British Caprotti' valve gear. The results with DUKE OF GLOUCESTER had proved most encouraging and it was decided that equipping thirty of the new Class 5s would allow the gear to be properly evaluated. In retrospect it is surprising that this was ever sanctioned, and Cox hints at resistance in the upper echelons of BR to any new steam developments. The nay-sayers had a point of course; there was experience enough with Caprotti gear going back a decade on the LMS and LMR after it. 'The Caprottis', 73125-73154, nevertheless duly appeared from Derby between July 1956 and June 1957 to works order No.9247. Oddly they did not all have the same tenders: 73125-73134 and 73145-73154 had the 1B, the other ten 73135-73144 the Type 1C. Great thought should have been given to the allocation of a new type such as this, with the gear wholly unfamiliar to any fitter. They should have been concentrated at one shed or at least in one Division with closely operating motive power depots, along with the existing LM examples and preferably 71000 too – which would mean in effect Crewe North and South – especially so since a new valve and piston examination shop was being prepared for the place. Instead the thirty Caprottis were divided, ten each, among the London Midland, Scottish and Western Regions – the last ten equipped with GW-type ATC. It was, you'd have to conclude, deliberate! It was vital, if the programme was to be conducted seriously, to concentrate them so that both fitting and footplate staff could properly familiarise themselves. Instead these men merely adapted to the new engines, learning as they went, helped when needed by one or two enthusiastic Derby men sent out when needed. Many sheds would send them home dead rather than fiddle with them.

Riddles seems to have been the champion of the Caprotti proposals. The gear had yielded improvements such as increased intervals between valve and piston exams; the two Black Fives, 44686 and 44687 of 1951 incorporated detail revisions and a new arrangement that was adopted for the BR ones. The LMS/BR Caprottis had been introduced with just as little thought to efficient operating and the problems experienced, especially the unfamiliarity of crews and fitters and the need for specialist men to come out from main works, though a relatively rare event, meant utilisation did not increase as it might.

Crosti Boiler?

Proposals for fitting Crosti boilers to BR Caprotti Class 5s thankfully came to nought. They emerged before enthusiasm for the Crosti boilered 9Fs had collapsed in face of the grim reality of dirt and cost. Happily this remained a 'might have been'.

Rugby and Road Tests

Like many Standards the new 4-6-0 was also tested at the Rugby plant and on the road. New 73008 in 1951 was found to be a less impressive steam raiser than had been hoped, confirming the initial verdicts coming in from the sheds. Minor modifications were made to the grate but the answer was perceived to be reduced blastpipe dimensions and 73030 with the said alterations proved the point in 1953; all engines had the blastpipe orifice altered from $5\frac{1}{8}$ inches to $4\frac{7}{8}$ inches.

Frames

Bar frames might have become central to British steam building had BR works been equipped to handle and machine them – that was apart from the extra cost; the BR Standards were not born into a cash-rich era. Money of course, or rather foreign exchange, was probably the main reason we got a new generation of steam locomotives rather than diesels in the first place. Cox had dreamed of bar frames, eliminating at last the cracking and constant patch and mend; bar frames, as perfected in the United States, lasted as long as the locomotive but there was nowhere to start in Britain, where there was no tradition of building, machining and

73131 brand new at Derby shed, 22 September 1956. The batch of ten that went to Shrewsbury oddly enough very largely replaced Walschaerts Class 5s which had gone to Shrewsbury from LM or Scottish Region sheds a few years before. In truth the status of Shrewsbury remained a bit enigmatic. It was really two sheds, a GW and LMS one side by side. It was 'rationalised' as one single depot in the WR Wolverhampton District about 1952 but in reality little changed operationally. So when we say the ten Caprottis 73125-73134 went to the Western Region, they may have really gone to the LMR, working to Manchester and being serviced at Patricroft for which shed they all upped sticks for after a couple of years anyway. R.J. Buckley, Initial Photographics.

Apart from having two cylinders rather than three, the British Caprotti valve gear as used on the Class 5s was exactly similar in principle to the arrangement on the 8P Pacific DUKE OF GLOUCESTER. This is 73144; on top of the cylinder casting is the cam box. The drive from the return arm* on the intermediate driving wheel translated circular movement in one direction, that is the crank on the centre wheel, to circular movement in a longitudinal direction via a bevel gearbox. The same thing happened at the other end of the shaft to drive the cam shaft, which was mounted transversely across the top on the cylinder in what was referred to as the cam box. The cams then drove the poppet valves via an arrangement of levers. The circular rod disappearing up towards the cab is the reversing rod and it controlled the scrolls that altered the position of the cams relative to the shaft that drove them, thus altering the valve events. The reversing rod drove via an intermediate gearbox that can be been seen above the slide bars and just below the foot framing. This stepped down the movement of the reversing gear, as while only one complete revolution of the reversing wheel was necessary to move the gear from full forward to full backward gear, the scrolls driving the camshaft mechanism were so arranged that even one complete turn of the wheel would have been too great. In the picture can just be seen the front exhaust valve stem behind the main steam pipe.

*Actually, to call the drive from the crankpin a 'return arm' is probably both misleading and a misnomer even if it was the official designation. The return crank of Walschaerts gear functioned quite differently – it imparted a swinging motion to the expansion link. With Caprotti gear the arm simply rotated a short spindle that activated the bevel gearing for the drive shaft. This spindle was concentric with the centre of the driving wheel, so 'drive arm' would be a much more logical description.

73149 on the turntable at St Rollox shed, 4 May 1957. The ten that went to St Rollox lived out their lives there, largely. They were withdrawn or transferred to other sheds where it was not long before they were withdrawn – without doing much you have to suspect. What on earth did Ayr make of 73145 for instance, when it arrived (if it ever did) on its allocation in September 1966, only to be withdrawn? There were no qualms with non-standard diesel classes of only a few years later, when any non-standard group was ruthlessly got rid off. J.L. Stevenson, courtesy Hamish Stevenson.

73150 on another turntable, at Dundee on 27 April 1957. Had there been more of a future in steam, then Caprotti gear would have been The Way Ahead. J. Robertson, www.transporttreasury.co.uk

A Caprotti in London; 73137 with its 17C plate is a Rowsley engine and on 13 July 1963 it is at Cricklewood shed; Rowsley acquired several but what the fitters made of them is anyone's business. Stephen Gradidge.

Caprotti 73137 on 18 February 1967; it might have been expected that the Caprottis would be withdrawn before the conventional engines but they seemed to survive just as well; rather better maybe. Not that they didn't suffer the usual indignities; 73137 was well-known in this twilight of its life for one of the more egregious home-made front numberplates; fortunately we are spared it in this view on the turntable at Patricroft though it will appear later in the book. Note twin lubricators on this right-hand side, of which more anon. I. Laidlaw, www.transporttreasury.co.uk

The Caprotti system of cams, rods and bevels could not generate the reciprocating motion so characteristic of Walschaerts motion so the mechanical lubricators could not be operated in the same way. They were driven instead off the rear driving wheel, as on the LMS Caprottis; there they are, positioned together by the firebox on 73151 at Dundee on 28 August 1965. This left no room under the running plate valence, which is why the piping of the exhaust steam injector is so prominent on the Caprotti engines. The lubricator drive rod comes off that crank on the rear axle – see also the pictures of 73138 and 73137. Stephen Gradidge.

handling such frames. Moreover they were more suited to wide firebox locomotives, not the traditional British narrow between the frames firebox. The only course was to make do with plate frames, finessed (if that is the right word) to minimise cracking and fracture after the latest advances seen under Bulleid for instance, with welded hornguides and the extensive use of cross stretchers. As it was, BR Standard frames were far from free of cracking/fracture and their working life was nothing like that offered by bar frames. Cox had to carry on dreaming of USA-style cast steel engine beds with integral cylinders; just as Britain felt unable to tackle this most modern of developments, the steam engine was beginning its headlong decline across the Atlantic.

Injectors
The high running plates allowed easy access to anything below the footplate, while pipe runs were carried invisibly behind the 'lip' of the running plate. A multitude of sins could thus be hidden even more completely than on an engine with conventional running plate. An advantage was that when the boiler was lifted the running plates went with it thus clearing the running gear. On the left-hand side was the live steam injector, a GWR type. In devising the Standards this had been judged markedly superior and Cox remarks on the odd fact that this injector was one feature Stanier did not import to the LMS, persisting with the Derby design which was not nearly as good. On the right-hand side was the Davies & Metcalfe exhaust steam injector with its delivery pipe rising vertically from the cone before it turned at right angles towards the clack valve at the front of the boiler.

Lamp Brackets
The original arrangement was conventional enough, three irons spaced along the front buffer beam and one at the top of the smokebox door. Those sent new to the Western Region had to have that Region's 'sideways on' irons so as to carry its lamp with the bracket on the side rather than the rear. When transferred out of the WR the lamp irons were made face on. Subsequent examples that found their way to the WR, to Shrewsbury, seem to have retained their conventional irons. If the shed concerned had been somewhere deep in the Western, like Laira, these surely would have been changed but Shrewsbury was old border country where half the allocation was LM in origin anyway. Moreover it would soon transfer back to the LMR. There was no shortage of lamps there of either ilk.

Those on the Southern Region had to have two additional brackets on the smokebox door to carry the route indicator discs.

About 1963 all top lamp brackets were ordered to be lowered for safety reasons, to avoid the electrocution of firemen when changing lamps or headboards. The top lamp shifted to the smokebox door and the middle buffer beam iron shifted a little to the right to be in line. The edict was ignored on the Southern Region, where smokebox doors were already a little crowded.

Driving Wheel Axles
The coupled wheels of the first thirty or so engines had hollow axles; the Britannias had suffered wheel movement on the axles, solved after much investigation and revised workshop practice when dealing with roller bearings. The problem did not manifest itself on the Class 5s but the hollow axles, as on the Pacifics, were plugged as a preventative measure. Thereafter solid axles were used which were indistinguishable from the plugged hollow ones.

Bearings
Timken roller bearings were fitted on all wheels, engine and tender, with manganese liners. There was a line of lineage in this going back to the LMS/BR Black Fives fitted with both Timken and Skefco bearings, not necessarily on all wheels.

Coupling Rods
The coupling rods of the new Standards were an attractive fluted design, but not massively solid. There was rod damage associated with the axle shifting in the Britannias and in a belt and braces approach (as Cox put it) the fluted rods were ordered to be superseded by tapered ('fish-belly') rectangular section ones. They appear new on 73050 onwards (April 1954) but were never 'retro-fitted' to the first fifty, which rather suggests that the fluted trousers

73082 lovely and new at Derby shed, destined for the Southern and eventual naming as CAMELOT and preservation after that, on 27 June 1955. Speedometer prominent because it's new and clean. Big 1B tender but no water scoop, '5' power classification, long lubricator reach rod, extra front irons on smokebox door (there were two extra lamp irons on the back of the tender too). R.J. Buckley, Initial Photographics.

And another beautiful black one destined for the Southern, at Derby shed two days later, on 29 June 1955. All of this batch, 73080-73089, were destined initially for Stewarts Lane. R.J. Buckley, Initial Photographics.

The air-braked Class 5s, 73030 and 73031 were not of great interest, for they were only so fitted for a year or so but these close-ups are just as useful for illustrating general features of the Walschaerts gear. On 73031 the extra fitments for the air brakes are the big cylinder by the firebox just visible to the left (an air reservoir for the train air brakes) and the lagged piping attached to the boiler cladding and looped round the pipe to the clack valve. The engines were steam braked and were equipped to work both vacuum and air braked trains. The smaller cylinder above the driver's head is the housing for a spring that connected to the reversing shaft. This made the driver's task easier when winding the reverser. This spring was present on all the class except those with Caprotti gear, which didn't need it. W. Webb, courtesy Rod Fowkes.

would have stayed up without the fish-belly belt and braces after all.

Sanding
Conventional steam sanding was used, to the front of the leading driving wheel and to the front and rear of the middle driving wheel, with two sandboxes either side.

Return Crank
The return crank was mounted on a square pin, LNER style. From the mid-1950s this was gradually replaced by a standard LMS-type four stud design, which was fitted from new, it would appear, from 73100. Many of the earlier ones got the new arrangement while a few, inevitably, never got the modification.

Running Plates
The BR Class 5s looked nothing like the Stanier Black Five lurking beneath and this was owed principally to the high running plate which was characteristic of most of the Standard tender classes. Many were aghast at the unnaturally high running plates; H.C. Casserley remarked of the only BR Standard to have a 'running plate of moderate height', the 78000 moguls, that it was thus 'the best proportioned of the new designs'. Yet to any foreign eyes they would still seem to possess those famously 'clean' British lines, uncluttered by sandboxes on the boiler top and other mortifications. The great advantage of course was the much easier access to all the running gear. The running plates were attached to the smokebox, boiler and firebox rather than the traditional frame mounting.

Lubrication
Mechanical lubricators delivered oil to the cylinders and valves via an atomiser. Enormous care had been taken in the design and layout of the lubrication system but worrying problems had appeared on the Britannias; some engines suffered, others didn't and some sheds reported problems while others didn't. The Class 5s with identical cylinder design and valve events presumably had their moments too, though they weren't driven to the same high speeds and outputs. The mechanical lubricators, one each side, were located behind the running plate, with access via a bolted cover. These covers were

Right-hand side of 73031 in 1953 with that big exhaust steam injector with its delivery pipe rising vertically and up under the from the cone before it turned at right angles towards the clack valve at the front of the boiler. Cantilevered cab floor clearly projecting rearwards on framing; the cut-out plate at the rear of the cab instead of the traditional fall plate is visible (see the picture of 73014 at Eastleigh being painted green for example) as is the projection of the tender coal shovelling plate, complete with shovel. It was the gap below in the absence of a fall plate that allowed the wind to rush in so disagreeably. Tarpaulin/rubber bellows/flexible screen attached to try to stem the draughts. Water supply pipe connection to the injector, running along the frame of the tender to the sieve box (unbolted periodically and washed out – had to be kept unfrozen in the depths of winter) where solids and the occasional fish – eels in particular seemed to find them rather congenial – were filtered out from the dirty water in the tender. W. Webb, courtesy Rod Fowkes.

73131 again, this time in workaday condition, waiting at Birmingham New Street, platform 3. Paul Chancellor Collection.

an encumbrance and were abandoned for ease of maintenance after a few months, so that most BR Class 5s never had the cover.

The Walschaerts Class 5s had a mechanical lubricator either side; the Caprottis could not provide the reciprocating motion necessary to operate them so both lubricators were sited on the right-hand side, in the running plate as usual but by the firebox and worked by a rod driven by a return crank attached to the rear crankpin – as on the LMS/LMR Caprotti locos.

Lubricator Drive Rod
A horizontal rod (on the Walschaerts engines, not the Caprotti ones) off the expansion pivot link operated a vertical rod which drove the lubricator. This vertical reach rod varied in length between engines and even on the sides of individual engines. They changed to a short reach rod, probably from the late 1950s and not before, seemingly indiscriminately, during works visits.

Chime Whistle
The whistle at first was sited behind the chimney, operated by Bowden cable running through the handrail on the right-hand boiler side and with a steam supply from a valve low down on the same right-hand side, on the smokebox. The whistle (worries developed that it could not be heard when the engines were working hard) was removed to a more conventional site on the firebox and replaced by a standard whistle half-way through production; you can never be entirely certain about these things but it seems to have come about from 73100 onwards – with the first Doncaster ones 1955-56, followed by the next in line from Derby at the end of 1955, in the earlier-numbered but later-built 73090 series. The cable operating the newly-sited whistle ran through the handrail, as before.

Names
It was entirely unexpected, but maybe the Southern Railway King Arthur class names were just too good not to perpetuate; thus it was that from 1959 a number of names from withdrawn Arthurs were given to Southern Region Class 5s. They are of course wonderful names, redolent of power, history, myth and romance, and so perfect for steam locomotives. By the same measure they'd be unthinkable today. Here they are with the dates (all plates fitted at Eastleigh Works except 73111):

73080 MERLIN
nameplates fitted w/e 4/2/61

73081 EXCALIBUR
nameplates fitted w/e 11/2/61

73082 CAMELOT
nameplates fitted w/e 15/8/59

73083 PENDRAGON
nameplates fitted w/e 16/10/59

73084 TINTAGEL
nameplates fitted w/e 31/10/59

73085 MELISANDE
nameplates fitted w/e 8/8/59

73086 THE GREEN KINIGHT
nameplates fitted w/e 12/12/59

73087 LINETTE
nameplates fitted w/e 27/5/61

73088 JOYOUS GARD
nameplates fitted w/e 6/5/61

73089 MAID OF ASTOLAT
nameplates fitted w/e 30/5/59

73110 THE RED KNIGHT
nameplates fitted w/e 23/1/60

73111 KING UTHER
nameplates fitted w/e 11/2/61 at Nine Elms shed

73112 MORGAN LE FAY
nameplates fitted w/e 2/4/60

73113 LYONESSE
nameplates fitted w/e 12/12/59

73114 ETARRE
nameplates fitted w/e 19/3/60

73115 KING PELLINORE
nameplates fitted w/e 30/1/60

Top. KING PELLINORE with little sandbox lid above.

Bottom. The Southern names were reminiscent of the original King Arthur ones but the middle bolts could have done with being countersunk!

73116 ISEULT
nameplates fitted w/e 15/9/62

73117 VIVIEN
nameplates fitted w/e 15/4/61

73118 KING LEODEGRANCE
nameplates fitted w/e 20/2/60

73119 ELAINE nameplates fitted w/e 13/6/59

Self Cleaning Smokebox
All of the Standard engines were fitted with this gear, of often questionable utility. It would be interesting to hear the reaction today, given modern environmental 'concerns' given that 'self-cleaning' simply means 'expelled to the atmosphere'. Not that the fine char could harm anyone; it settled straight away and was not injurious to lungs. As put in *The Book of the Britannia Pacifics* (Irwell Press) it was after all, 'only fertiliser.' Self-cleaning was denoted by the SC plate on the bottom of the smokebox door, normally under the shedplate. Pioneered by the LMS in the previous decade, the self cleaning screens had the principal advantage in that the build-up of char in the base of the box was avoided; this in turn avoided the onerous daily task (though it had to be done eventually of course) of emptying the smokebox by shovel. Burning of the smokebox door was also avoided – mostly. The self-cleaning apparatus was removed both officially and unofficially, to an unknown extent.

Speedometers
The standard Smith-Stone speedometer was fitted new from 73030 onwards and the equipment later appeared on some of the earlier thirty.

ATC/AWS
The BR AWS (Automatic Warning System) was some years in the future when the first Standards came out, though those Class 5s destined for the Western Region (the 'middle ten' Caprottis) had the local GWR ATC (Automatic Train Control) fitted at Swindon when delivered. AWS began to appear on the other engines from 1959 but by no means all of the Class 5s were fitted. The WR ATC was removed before the locos left the Western Region and, it seems, they never got the BR gear once on the LMR. Cost of fitting to an individual Class 5 came to just over £300 per engine which, as a percentage, was not trivial. The BR gear was characterised by the battery box; it held two batteries and was the one feature to be found on engines from 0-4-4Ts to Pacifics across every Region, aside from the Western of course. On the Class 5s it was vertical, under the driver's side of the cab (left-hand looking forward) though the reservoir cylinders, often placed on the running plate (particularly on the LMR) were invisible. The most obvious feature was the protector plate behind the front drawhook, below the buffer beam.

The BR running plate with its downward lip was handy to hide a multitude of sins including the AWS conduit from the receiver at the front to the cab, which was hidden behind the lip. With an oblivious eye to central direction that gives meaning to the engine picker's life, some engines had the conduit tacked – see the joyfully untidy example of 73078 at Crianlarich for instance – to *the outside* of the lip of the running plate. Was the fitter sacked, or sent for re-education?

Slidebars
The Gresley/Bulleid three-bar type with under slung crosshead was adopted; as described in *The Book of the Britannia Pacifics*: 'The 1¼in. gap for the travel of the crosshead was opened up and extended for a length of ten inches at the cylinder end of the slidebars. This was done so that with the front cover removed and the small end disconnected and dropped, the crosshead could be pushed forward to expose the piston for examination. The advantages were that the slidebar assembly and piston rod cotter could remain undisturbed.'

Ashpan
The ashpan had three separate hoppers and was thus, like the much bigger Britannia ashpan, a 'complicated three-dimensional affair'. It was made of corrosion-resistant copper steel plate. The contents were emptied by a lever operated mechanism outside.

Rocking Grates
The 'Rocking Grate Committee' deemed rocking grates essential and all the BR Standards were so equipped. It was also possible for the fireman to rock the grate somewhat while running; 'stops' were fitted to ensure the grate really was only rocked, not completely opened, when out on the road. Nevertheless, grates were not delicate things and, corroded and clinkered, they could stick open, so it had to be done gingerly. At the shed the bars could be

Brand new 73085 stands out amidst the scruffy 0-6-0s at Derby shed, 5 August 1955. Fish belly rectangular section coupling rods now of course (compare to the fluted rods of the earlier ones like 73031). It would later be named MELISANDE. R.J. Buckley, Initial Photographics.

A few weeks later, the future LINETTE is the latest BR Class 5 to take its place at Derby shed for running in, before heading off south. R.J. Buckley, Initial Photographics.

The Book of the BR Standard Class 5 4-6-0s

Original Type 1 tender, cab floor cantilevered rearwards, on 73000 late on in its life at Woodford Halse shed, 23 August 1964. The 'flexible screen' has come and gone and by now, with much slower jobs and a general air of 'it won't be long now' the old complaints of draughts did not have so much force. Stephen Gradidge.

'rocked' almost through 90 degrees so that everything would fall into the ashpan and through its bottom flap doors straight into the pit.

Snow Plough/ Front Vacuum Pipe
Some Scottish (actually, only those at Perth) Class 5s were fitted up for snow ploughs which required the raising of the front vacuum pipe above the buffer beam. There were also prominent brackets below the buffer beam, which were sometimes removed along with the ploughs in the summer – or the non-snow season anyway.

Cabs and Tenders - Draught Excluding
The tender type, capacity and allocation for each group of locomotives is given in the earlier Building and Basic Details table. Experience gained with the first Britannias was painfully repeated in the case of the Class 5s. Take the mating of the tender to the cab; beginning with 73000 the whole of the cab floor was attached to the engine, which abolished (precipitately, in the event) the traditional fall-plate between engine and tender. There was a 'pillar handrail' from the rear of the cab roof to the extended cab floor; the traditional door, in two halves, spring loaded with one hinged on the tender and one on the cabside, were thus absent. This arrangement caused problems for at speed, a powerful backdraught could be generated through the gap, just as on the Pacifics with consequent draught, dust and noise. Rubberised canvas 'bellows' or 'draught curtains' were fitted, optimistically termed 'flexible screens'. They became slack and hanging, awful looking rags in service and were never wholly successful. When the Type 1 tender was superseded, from 73050 onwards, more traditional arrangements were instituted, with fall plate to an extended tender floor and doors attached to the tender. The Southern modified the cabs of its Class 5s (or the original twenty allocated, at least, 73080-73089 and 73110-73119) by constructing solid metal draught screens at the rear, Bulleid-fashion.

Air Brakes
Air brakes were fitted to Britannias 70043 and 70044 when new, for trials to determine the relative merits of air as opposed to vacuum, with an eye (a very optimistic one – the cost would have been colossal) to future standardisation on one or the other. 73030 and 73031 also came out new in June-July 1953 with the air brake gear – they were fitted with two compressors, Westinghouse driver's brake valve, main and auxiliary reservoirs on each side. One test involved 73031 in December 1953 with 52 empty (new!) mineral wagons and a brake van Toton-Bedford and presumably there were variations on this. The work was conducted from Toton shed, though the locos were never officially allocated there. The gear seems to have been removed in 1954.

T.I.A.
Traitement Integral Armand had long been in use on the Southern; the Pacifics had steel fireboxes and they had the advantage over copper in cost and ease of manufacture but water treatment was essential. It had been standard procedure on the SNCF and in the United States for years and was rather more 'scientific' than most procedures familiar at running sheds, requiring some firm adherence to daily schedules of upkeep. Scale-forming compounds in hard water were precipitated out as a soft mud, eliminating the hardness of the water and stopping corrosion. A simpler and cheaper BR system of briquettes replaced the TIA apparatus from about 1956. All the BR Standards had copper fireboxes because water quality across the country could not be assured. The Southern decided its Class 5s would nevertheless benefit from water treatment; they were duly adapted, as were Class 5s which subsequently arrived on the region. A small yellow circle on the cabside below the number indicated TIA, and later a yellow triangle was applied to show that the BR water treatment was installed instead. Both were often invisible under the grime.

Steps at Front
These were bolted to the plunging running plate at the front, either side of the frames. They varied in height, Doncaster placing them slightly higher

Type 1 tender behind 73003, screens compact and functioning, on a down excursion leaving Leicester Midland on 21 April 1956. Peter Groom.

73050 of Willesden Exhibition fame with inset Type 1G tender (the 5,000 gallon 1A with fall plate and gangway doors) at Heaton Mersey in April 1964. With the exception of the Class 2 2-6-0s which had conventional arrangements, all the Standards turned out new in 1954 had the altered rear end layout to combat the excessive draughts of the original cab/tender configuration. www.transporttreasury.co.uk

73059 at Polmadie about 1955 with one of the new tenders, this time classified 1H; they were essentially the BR1 tenders but with a fall plate and gangway doors. The modified cabs had a noticeably different look and were distinguished by the absence of that distinctive handrail pillar running vertically down from the rear edge of the cab roof. J. Robertson, www.transporttreasury.co.uk

Type 1C tender on 73075 new at Derby shed on 21 April 1955. It looked the same as the Type 1B but had a coal capacity of 9 tons rather than the 7 tons of the latter. Both tenders looked identical except for the additional coal space partition plate of the 1B which reduced coal capacity. Peter Groom.

New 1C tenders on 73067 and 73072 at Derby on 25 October and 10 December respectively in 1954 – so clean that (on the original prints at least) the numbers can be read, 1006 and 1011. R.J. Buckley, Initial Photographics.

Life on a Type 1C tender; Southampton Central, May 1965. K. Pullen, www.transporttreasury.co.uk

73096 blowing off in the rain and waiting for the signal at Shrewsbury in the 1950s affords a good view of the big nine ton Type 1C tender with its ladders, lifting rings, brackets and patches. The lower oval plate gives the water capacity, the upper oblong one the tender number and year of building. www.transporttreasury.co.uk

73117 at Nine Elms, 10 September 1966. Some removed screens from the self cleaning smokebox apparatus on the front running plate. Loco very dirty; AWS, VIVIEN plate gone, tender emblem now a ghostly shadow, simple '5' above the number, yellow water treatment triangle – a minor miracle that we can see both. For the first time we encounter the short vertical reach rod to the lubricator. The tender has the quite distinctive look of the Type 1F. Only ten of the BR Class 5s were equipped with this version, which was more generally familiar from the Eastern Region's 9F 2-10-0s; the 1F had 7 tons coal capacity but an increased water capacity of 5,625 gallons. The latter was particularly useful on the Southern Region, lacking water troughs as it did; accordingly the Region's ten 1F tenders did not have water scoops. Peter Groom.

73118 also with 1F tender makes for a curious contrast with 73117; it stands in the same Nine Elms shed yard, a few yards away but it is a whole decade before. On 14 October 1956 73118 is barely a year old but has got very scruffy indeed, so that it hardly looks better than 73117 in 1966. Nevertheless these Nine Elms Class 5s were doing good work on semi-fasts out of Waterloo, supplanting Urie Arthurs and so on. Long lubricator reach rod, first tender emblem, KING LEODEGRANCE nameplate not yet fixed, markedly larger cab numbers than 73117, no water treatment symbol (presumably not so equipped yet) and 5P 5F (the P and the F smaller than the 5...). R.J. Buckley, Initial Photographics.

Caprotti 73136 on the turntable at Holyhead, 13 August 1964; emblem entirely obscured under grime. The coal capacities of the 1B and 1C (7 and 9 tons respectively) were determined by the positioning of the space plate between the front and rear of the coal space, as shown here; on the B version it was quite a bit further forward. The drawback was that the rear portion was effectively 'dead' space which very quickly filled with coal that could not be used. It deteriorated to unusable quality and encouraged corrosion. Hamish Stevenson.

than Derby. One or two even acquired both high and low steps; they fitted pre-existing bolt holes after all, so the section of running plate itself must have been changed.

Cab Roof Lifting Brackets
Eastleigh fixed four lifting brackets to the cab roofs for ease of handling when dismantled during overhauls.

Tablet Catchers
Several Class 5s working on the Somerset and Dorset were equipped with the near-invisible Whitaker tablet catcher, bolted low down on the tender at the left-hand side. It was the custom to loan locomotives to Bath Green Park for summer working on the S&D and the apparatus would be taken off and stored for the winter when it was time for the locos to be returned. A number of Scottish locos were also equipped with tablet mechanisms.

Tender Step Plate
The sloping top edge of the BR1 and 1A tenders were hazardous to men clambering about when watering and a foot step platform and bracket was added to give a safer, flat surface. The first few were soon modified and the rest were built with the plates in place.

Liveries
BR lined 'LNW' (usually ascribed to the influence of Riddles, a man with an LNW background) mixed traffic black was the livery of the BR Class 5s; grey, cream and red lining on the cab and tender. 73000 at first ran with a 'panel' of lining on the running plate valence which was afterwards revised to a simpler strip, along the lower edge of the valence. There were two red lines for each boiler band and the cylinder casing too. Individual locos over the years throw up some minor variations in height, extent, omission and so on.

The complications of the Caprotti cylinders meant they had to forego the twin lines of red on the cylinder casing.

As Regional boundaries changed the Western Region acquired BR Class 5s off the LMR, losing some of them again later as other territory was ceded to the LMR and also to the Southern. The WR repainted a number of these Walschaerts-fitted Class 5s in BR lined dark green as a matter of routine. Lining was orange and black with a single orange line at the bottom of the running plate 'lip'. The green ones that ended up on other Regions while still WR locos, kept the green, touched up in the main. Eastleigh introduced a variant, in that the lining on the running plate 'lip' was a panel. It was the owning Region which, in theory, specified the livery which explains why green WR Class 5s emerged form 'foreign works' still in green – but then there was the strange case of 73014...

This appears to be the list of engines – nineteen – painted green at Swindon or Wolverhampton:
73001, 73003, 73012, 73015, 73018, 73021, 73024, 73026, 73027, 73031, 73034, 73035, 73036, 73037, 73054, 73068, 73093, 73096, 73097.

This is explained by the WR's local policy. The others that got green applied over black (not as a repaint/touch up) at Eastleigh, Doncaster and Darlington were 73014, 73023, 73029, 73032, 73040, 73049, 73051, 73090, 73091, 73092, 73094, 73095 and 73098. The likeliest explanation is that Swindon was responsible for the shopping proposals for these engines, even if working on another Region and simply specified green. Maybe it was Swindon's revenge on Riddles and his beloved LNW black!

Electrification flashes were ordered to be applied from 1960 though neither the

The London Midland's very own 73014 (chime whistle replaced by standard whistle on firebox; electrification flashes in place) at Eastleigh in January-March 1964, getting a coat of BR dark green. Had they simply run out of black paint that week? 73037, already in green, had arrived from the Western at the same time – did someone merely assume the 73000s were painted green? The owning Region would foot the bill for overhauls in 'foreign' works and would have placed the shopping proposal; this in theory would have stipulated the livery to be applied, assuming it was a repair that included a full re-paint. The LMR would most definitely not have specified green! Lining set up on cabside; panel on running plate valence. It had come from Willesden and went back to the LM in this shimmering form to dazzle the eyes of the natives at Bletchley. Eastleigh did the same with 73029 from its own Weymouth shed and with three more, 73040, 73049 and 73051. The latter two were from the WR but 73040 was from Croes Newydd, by now firmly under LM control. The explanation can only be that Swindon was still responsible for its shopping proposal – this would also explain 73029 from Eastleigh's own back yard. Notice the engine sits on valve setting rollers, with connecting rod temporarily fitted. J.G. Walmsley, www.transporttreasury.co.uk

Bristol Barrow Road's 73068 a long way from home, at New England; the date is not known but the Class 5's home shed had got its WR code in February 1958 and left in September 1962 so it is somewhere in that 4½ year period. The occasion is almost certainly a works visit in May 1960, when Doncaster reapplied or touched up its *green* livery applied by Swindon two years before. Its condition suggests it is running in from Doncaster and will be on its way back home soon. The view shows well the removable panel on the sloping front for access to pistons and piston valves; a design team less concerned with aesthetics might have left this blank. Imagine the outcry if all the BR Standards had looked a bit like the Ivatt Class 4 2-6-0s! There again, where would you have put the steps? The projection on the front of the cylinder cover is the pressure relief valve, to relieve any excessive pressure or water trapped in the cylinder. Photograph B. Richardson, www.transporttreasury.co.uk

Southern nor the Western seem to have bothered overmuch.

Power Classification
This was placed above the cabside number and for such a simple thing seems chaotic in its application. The BR Class 5s were officially, it would seem, 5MT – so far as head office was concerned at least. That is, they were power class five and intended for mixed traffic. LMR works used the LMS '5' on its own, Doncaster didn't bother, at least with the first and other batches for the Scottish Region. The second batch for the Southern Region had the simple '5', at least at first though it may have been done by Eastleigh; when deliveries for the Scottish Region resumed from Doncaster, the '5' disappeared again. After that anything could appear. The power classification above the number was thus variable; the 'correct' Eastleigh classification for instance was 5P/5FA but they all got 5P 5F or 5P/5F and in the last years, even when overhauled at Eastleigh, they got the plain '5'.

Cab Numbers
The Scots (Cowlairs and St Rollox) and Darlington (mostly) applied ten inch cab side numbers rather than the eight inch applied everywhere else, for no obvious reason – both sizes were of equal utility. Whether a job lot of transfers found itself to Eastleigh or it is an optical illusion, some SR Class 5s cab numbers in the 1950s look very much like the ten inch version...

Buffer Beam Indications
Doncaster and St Rollox had a habit of painting the class designation on the buffer beam and some Class 5s were so observed. Various motive power depot names appeared over the years, painted on the front buffer beam.

Western Region Route Availability Disc
Most if not all Western Region Class 5s had a two inch disc applied below the number on the cab side indicating the route availability; in this case red for their maximum axle loading. They disappeared on transfer away from the WR, first under grime, then under paint.

Eastfield's 73105 at Haymarket on 10 March 1956. There was room forward to bring most of the piston out without removing the sloping running plate at the front. The cylinders were steel, with cast iron liners; this was American practice, unusual in the UK and periodic replacement of the liners imparted almost limitless life to the cylinder casting. The driver did not need a pit in the oiling of the BR Class 5s, or for most of the BR Standards in fact – an enormous advantage of two cylinders. Note row of grease nipples under the cylinder drain cock gear; these would feed the bogie suspension arrangements through a series of pipes. On the top of the steam chest is the anti-vacuum valve, which allowed both ends of the cylinder to be connected together when the engine was coasting, thus preventing a vacuum being created and ashes and cylinder from the smokebox etc, being drawn into the valve chest. Above the running plate on the side of the smokebox is the large and small vacuum ejector, for creating the brake vacuum. Two holes at top of cylinder casing – not a general feature... J. Robertson, www.transporttreasury.co.uk

A Mixed Reception?

Scottish Region Experiences with the BR Class 5 4-6-0s, 1951-1952

Perhaps the most meaningful evaluation of the BR Class 5s came in 1951-52, as originally recounted by Kevin Pile in our magazine, British Railways Illustrated, April 1998:

Not all the Regions, by any means, it seems, took the trouble to carry out protracted evaluations of the new Standard engines they were expected to operate from 1951. The Scottish Region did do so, however, and the results survive among E.S. Cox's papers now held at the National Railway Museum, York. The following notes are distilled from this Report, from the Motive Power Superintendent, Glasgow, dated 28 February 1952 and entitled *Report on the Performance of the BR Standard Class 5 4-6-0 Mixed Traffic Locomotive in the Scottish Region*.

At the time, there were five of the BR Standard Class 5 4-6-0s allocated to the Scottish Region; four were at Perth shed and one, No.73008, had been used for testing purposes outside the Region. The four Perth engines came new from Derby to Scotland and building dates and mileages since new were as shown in the small table.

From the outset the engines were utilised continuously on express passenger trains on the Glasgow/Perth/Aberdeen, Carstairs/Perth/Aberdeen sections of the line dealing with trains in many cases up to the maximum Class 5 loading, booked at point-to-point timings which called for sustained high speeds over fairly difficult stretches.

As the engines went into service, it was decided that each one would be allocated to two sets of top link enginemen only, and, where necessary, the engine diagrams and the composition of the enginemen's links at Perth were adjusted to allow for this. This arrangement, as everyone was aware, overcame many of the disabilities arising from lack of individual care. As a result, the engines were worked more or less by a small group of experienced, capable enginemen. Only the record for 73005 and 73006 survive, but they are sufficient to illustrate the sort of maintenance problems encountered – see below.

The items listed are those which arose during routine maintenance and examination; the experience is summarised as follows, a) – g).

(a) Cylinders, Pistons and Piston Valves
Rapid wear was found to be taking place on the piston rings, piston head carriers, piston valve rings and piston valve liners of the new engines. The Scottish Region investigators were, at this time, in the dark along with everyone else and at first it was thought that the problem could be remedied by fitting non-slip thimbles to the cylinder mechanical lubricators, thereby increasing the oil feed to each point.

This failed to yield any great improvement; 73007 for instance had to be specially proposed for the attention of the Mechanical and Electrical Engineer at St Rollox for removal of the piston valve liners. This was puzzling for the mechanical lubricator on the new engines delivered more oil to the fore-end than was the case with the Black 5s then in long and familiar use.

The author of the Report noted: *In my opinion, part of the trouble is the method of operation of the atomiser, and I consider that it is quite possible for a driver to run*

No.	Built	Date to Perth	Approx total mileage to date
73005	20.6.51	11.7.51	40,000
73006	28.6.51	20.7.51	40,310
73007	9.7.51	26.7.51	46,000
73009	19.7.51	9.8.51	39,600

Engine No.73005, Tender No.799

11.7.51	6 superheater tubes expanded because of leakage.
14.7.51	Reported off the beat
23.7.51	Left big end hot (remetalled)
28.7.51	Reported off the beat in expansion
29.7.51	Tested for not steaming (water test - no defects)
6.8.51	Reversing wheel handle broken (Renewed)
12.8.51	Left piston valve rings examined (Good)
20.8.51	No 1 and No 2 exam 10,482 miles. Tender brake handle seized
22.8.51	Re-valve set and oil feeds increased
23.8.51	Piston rings renewed, atomiser steam valve springs renewed. Oil cups fitted to piston rods. (Mr Fisher, Derby in attendance)
28.8.51	Reversing Wheel Handle broken (renewed)
3.10.51	Tender brake screw seized (shaft removed)
6.10.51	No 3 Exam 20,156 miles
24.10.51	No 4 Exam 23,890 miles Atomiser springs renewed (supplied by St Rollox) Mr Fisher, Derby, in attendance
8.11.51	No 5 exam 26,799 miles. Tested for not steaming (no defects)
2.12.51	Right big end hot (bush loose in eye of rod)
6.12.51	No 6 exam 31,194 miles
31.12.51	Right eccentric crank bent (repairs at St Rollox)
16.1.52	Smokebox plates displaced
21.1.52	Special Proposal submitted. Wheels rubbing frame.

Engine No.73006, Tender No.800

28.7.51	Left big end hot (remetalled)
2.8.51	Brick arch renewed
4.8.51	Regulator valve not closing (adjusted)
17.8.51	Atomiser steam valve springs renewed
19.8.51	Brick arch repairs No 1 Exam
31.8.51	Piston valves to test (R valve 2 rings front head renewed. R valve 1 ring back head renewed) Atomiser springs renewed
5.9.51	Piston rings renewed
7.9.51	Right big end hot (remetalled)
12.9.51	Valves reset, piston carrier bars renewed
13.9.51	Left coupling rod knuckle pin bush renewed at No 2 Examination 14,384 miles
15.9.51	Left big end hot (remetalled)
26.9.51	Mech. lubricator feeds increased
6.10.51	No 3 Exam 19,629 miles
24.10.51	No 4 Exam (Mr Fisher, Derby, in Attendance)
10.4.51	No 5 Exam
21.11.51	Reversing lever balance spring belt broken en route. Waiting material until 3.12.61
14.1.52	Exhaust Injector defective. Sent to M & EE St Rollox

What a way to treat a bearing! The return crank eccentric is mounted on a square pin, LNER style. With 73100 in the mid-1950s this began to be replaced by a standard LMS-type four stud design. Many of the earlier ones got the new arrangement while a few, inevitably, never got it. The sandboxes are invisible and the delivery pipes descend behind the frames to reappear underneath. In front of the middle of the rear connecting rod is a cylindrical component; a hefty iron bar is inserted into this to operate the front ashpan hopper door. Good view of the regulator rodding.

73000 in Doncaster works, 11 January 1959. The chalked marks could be anything as reminders to staff. As the engine does not appear to have had a boiler lift perhaps the message INSERT IN BOTTOM LINER refers to one of those at the bottom of the smokebox - clearly the steam pipe has been renewed. www.transporttreasury.co.uk

for some distance with the atomiser inoperative, especially when his attention is taken up with adjusting the reversing gear and observing conditions outside the engine cab. Considering that the closing of the regulator invariably takes place while travelling at high speeds and that the temperature of metal of the piston valve liners at this time is very high, the engine does not require to run a very great distance before the oil film is broken down. I consider that the determining factor as to whether the atomiser is working or not should be whether the engine is in motion or not, rather than whether the regulator is open or shut. In other words, a system similar to the ex-LMS practice whereby the atomiser steam supply is controlled by the opening or closing of the cylinder cocks would give more efficient fore-end lubrication.

A further point arises in connection with the lubricator of the piston rod. In the arrangement on the new engines oil is fed from the mechanical lubricator (engine oil) direct to a swab box filled with worsted which is attached to the piston gland. Continual trouble was experienced with the piston rod packing blowing and it is felt that this was due to lack of lubrication of the piston rod. To rectify this, arrangements were made to fit additional brass oil cups (No.4 freight slidebar type) with siphon feed direct on to the piston rod and since this was done no further cases of piston packing blowing have been reported.

(b) Wheels, Axles and Axleboxes

The new 73000 engines were fitted throughout with Timken Roller Bearing Axleboxes, those of the engine being of the solid cannon type box and of the tender the separate axlebox type. These gave no trouble whatever in service. On engine 73005 it was found that the left trailing wheel was rubbing on the main frame but on removing the wheels from the engine, examination revealed that this rubbing was in no way dangerous. It was caused by the inside plate of the trailing wheel balance weight coming into contact with the frame when the engine rolled on its springs, the clearance when level between the balance weight plate and the frame being only half an inch. Opportunity was taken to examine the horn gap and axlebox horn sizes when the wheels of No.73005 were out and in no case was there any sign of excessive wear. The total end play on the axlebox fitted to the trailing axle was also checked and found to be within the laid down limits. The sanding gear as fitted was found to be very efficient, throwing 'an ample supply' of sand to each wheel.

(c) Motion, Coupling and Connecting Rods

In these first few months, the Scottish Region experienced no serious failures of any of the motion parts or of the coupling and connecting rods, though there had been seven cases of hot big ends. The bushes as fitted to the coupling and connecting rods were found to suffer considerable wear, however, and several had to be renewed. On many occasions bushes became slack in the eye of the rods; this, Scottish Region experience suggested, was due to the thinner shell of bronze left on these bushes as compared with the LMS Class 5s. The comparison was to recur repeatedly.

A further source of trouble was the brass knuckle pin bush fitted on the BR engines. This bush had a tendency to work slack in the eye of the rod and once the oil hole became displaced from its proper position, rapid wear ensued, necessitating in most cases a complete renewal of the bush concerned. Scottish advice was that steel bushes should be substituted. Two cases occurred of the reversing shaft balance spring breaking. This would appear to have been caused by the spring chafing on the guide and could be avoided, it was thought, 'by the adoption of a spring of stiffer action'.

The LNER/Bulleid slidebar and crosshead, and the heroic deposits that always built up on these components. The slidebars are fixed to the frame only, and not the cylinders too. Loosening the castle nut on the crosshead released a gudgeon pin so that the piston rod and piston could be eased forward of the cylinder for examination. Other Standard classes to the more restricted L1 loading gauge had the more conventional LMS-style arrangement with slidebars above and below the crosshead. Widened leading end of slidebar gap can be seen ahead of normal travel. Small oil cup at leading end of slidebars for lubricating piston rod. Peter Groom.

Eastleigh and 73022 under repair. The wheel at the front on the smokebox rim operates a valve for the tube cleaning lance: connect lance, hold away from body, open valve and steam emits. Place in tubes etc. One of the D6500 Type 3 diesels behind. B. Richardson, www.transporttreasury.co.uk

(d) Boiler and Smokebox

The performance of the boilers as fitted to the new engines was 'reasonably good' and few repairs had to be carried out. There were several instances of leaking superheater flue tubes and on one occasion, displacement of the self-cleaning smokebox plates occurred. Latterly, the top feed clack valve seatings began to work slack and the method of fixing them, it was thought, should receive consideration 'since the carrying out of repairs to this item at the Motive Power Depots gives endless trouble'. The rocking grate and hopper ashpan arrangement worked well, giving no trouble either in operation or during routine maintenance.

(e) Engine cab, mountings and superstructure

'There is no question' the Report says, 'that the layout of the controls on the new Class 5 engines meets with universal approval'. The positioning of the regulator handle, brake handle, reversing screw handle, blower handle, sander handle, vacuum ejector controls and cylinder cock control on the Driver's side and of the damper controls and all injector controls on the Fireman's side left little to be desired. The 'WR' type gauge frames and mountings in the event proved popular, for they gave a positive indication of the boiler water level at all times, 'due no doubt to the efficiency of the packing of the drain cock eliminating any tendency to blow through and thus give a false reading'.

The front cab windows were considered an improvement and (a factor I've not seen before) their position, at an angle to the longitudinal centre line of the engine, eliminated firebox glare 'completely'. The question of comfort in the cab, however, arose almost from the first. See *g) Performance in Traffic* below.

(f) Tender

The Report tried to be even-handed about the new tender - it had 'several good features' of which the increased water capacity was 'outstanding', and the hand brake and water pick up handles, it was thought, were conveniently positioned. The shovelling plate, however, was found by experiment to be too high: 'for convenient handling of the firing shovel it should be at the same level as the firehole door. The arrangement whereby the shovelling plate sloped to a depth of approximately 6in., some 4ft. from the opening, did not work well. This, coupled with the slope of the bunker bottom plates, did not materially assist the coal to run forward to the shovel, and presented a real inconvenience to the fireman when the supply of coal in the tender began to 'go back'. Scottish experience was that firemen were forced to clamber into the new BR1 tender much sooner and more frequently than with the older ex-LMS 4,000 gallon type.

Tender windows were a new feature, and one that was not appreciated. On the Scottish Region, the 4-6-0s would seldom be called on to do much running tender first and, presaging the bigger tenders which were later supplied, the Scottish Region put in a plea for something more akin to the Stanier tenders it was used to: ...*a straight sided tender of the 4,000 gallon type would have been more suitable, giving a considerable amount of extra coal space and allowing for the bunker plates to be so designed as to run the coal forward to the shovelling plate as it is used.*

(g) Performance in Traffic

The new 4-6-0s were found to be extremely fleet both on the level and on downhill stretches and the suspension such that a comfortable ride was always assured. Working on the up grade, however, the engines did not appear to have the power of the ex-LMS Black 5s, irrespective of the position of the reversing gear and the regulator. 'In consequence' it was stated, they 'had to be worked hard to maintain point-to-point bookings'. The normal method of working the engines was 25-30% cut-off with regulator approximately half open; 'it is under these conditions' the papers record, 'that the best work is done'. Whilst the engines appeared to be free-steaming when first put into service, difficulties soon manifested themselves, and even after six months or more no definite cause had been found. General opinion was that the engines did not steam so freely as the existing LM Class 5s. It was discussed thus: *To obtain best results, the coal must be of good quality and the controlled method of firing adopted. Indications are that the trouble is at the smokebox end and the question of the performance of the self cleaning apparatus is being closely looked into.*

The familiar objections to the cab arrangements surfaced almost immediately, and was put rather more forcefully than has been seen before: '*A matter for very serious consideration lies in the fact that when these engines are running, a draught is projected from both sides across the engine's footplate and in severe weather this renders conditions in the cab most uncomfortable and completely nullifies from the enginemen's point of view the advantages of the new cab layout.*'

General opinion was that the draught originated under the locomotive and was directed up the front plate of the tender. In addition to this, the fact that the front plate of the tender had square corners and was of such a width as to project beyond the cab into the slipstream, diverted (it seemed) a strong current of air directly across the footplate. To remedy this, it was suggested that the corners of the tender be rounded off, as in the ex-LMS Standard 4,000 gallon tender. The engines had run only some 40,000 miles since new, yet when working heavily with a 20-30% cut-off and full regulator, a distinct cab vibration and a very pronounced knock developed. This vibration gave every indication of axlebox knock and there were fears that, should it continue at such a rate, the desired aim of 100,000 miles between shoppings would be imperilled.

In order to record the performance of one of the new BR Standard Class 5 engines, two trips were made from Glasgow Buchanan Street to Aberdeen with the 10.0am ex-Glasgow and from Aberdeen to Perth with the 5.30pm ex-Aberdeen. The engines working these trains on the two days concerned, the 21st and 22nd February 1952, were Perth's Black 5 No.45365 and BR No.73009 on the respective days. 45365 underwent an Intermediate repair at St Rollox Works on 30th November 1951, having run some 10,000 until the date of the comparison. Apart from a considerable knock on the trailing axleboxes it was in good mechanical condition. Coal and water consumption were *(table opposite)*.

Mixed Reception

The coal consumption was arrived at by allowing 9lb coal per shovel since both engines were coaled 'over the flap'. The evaporation ratios derived would seem to indicate that the Black 5 was a better producer of steam per pound of fuel consumed on the grate, and the figures for coal consumption per ton mile worked would indicate that the new

45365
10.0am ex-Buchanan Street to Aberdeen, 153 miles
*Coal consumption = 7,956lb = 52.0lb/mile
Water consumption = 6,400 galls = 41.8 galls/mile
Evaporation ratio = 8
Coal consumption (ton miles) = 0.155*

5.30pm ex-Aberdeen, 90 miles
*Coal consumption 4,446lb = 49.3lb/mile
Water consumption 3,850 galls = 42.7 galls/mile
Evaporation ratio = 8.67
Coal consumption (ton miles) = 0.145*

73009
10.0am ex-Buchanan Street to Aberdeen, 153 miles
*Coal consumption = 8,145lb = 53.2lb/mile
Water consumption = 4,650lb = 30.4 galls/mile
Evaporation ratio = 5.72
Coal consumption (ton miles) = 0.184*

5.30pm ex-Aberdeen, 90 miles
*Coal consumption = 4,248lb = 47.2lb/mile
Water consumption = 3,100 gall s = 34.5 galls/mile
Evaporation ratio = 7.32 =
Coal consumption (ton miles) 0.137*

engine was *not* a more economical proposition from a load hauling point of view than its predecessor. So, unpalatable news for Riddles and Cox, though from a mechanical efficiency point of view the new engine seemed to have the advantage, requiring less steam to carry out a similar amount of work.

A mixed blessing, then, really, so far as the Scottish Region was concerned, and indeed it is not hard to see in its tone and import, however professional, balanced and polite the paper is, more than a hint that the Black 5s the Region already had in abundance would 'do perfectly well thank you'. Indeed, from its careful testing, this was a judgement the Region had every right - a duty even - to make. Yet the BR team had not particularly set out to *better* the Black 5

73053 down to the bare bones at Swindon; note the mechanical lubricator and sandbox feed left high and dry. Stanier 2-6-0 behind.

Above. **The BR Class 5s were seldom clean except after overhaul; most of the time they looked like this; scruffy 73010 at Woodford Halse shed on 23 August 1964. Note that the pipe (this is true of both sides) from the injectors to the clack valves atop the boiler front do not in fact run neatly behind the running plate 'lip' but instead 'emerge' to run on top – this is often not particularly obvious in photographs. Stephen Gradidge.**

to any great degree, though of course where possible detail improvements were seen, then they were pursued. Oddly, the success of the BR 5MT 4-6-0 lay in the fact that it was *not worse* than the Black 5 and even more vitally still, the same could be said on all the other Regions, whatever the 'rival' engines might be. Cox and the designers of the BR range were, as he said, 'committed to develop the best all-rounders…'

Below. **73003 in fairly deplorable nick, at Oxley on 6 July 1965. It even has the short-lived bracket for the name of the driver, which was fitted to many LM locos but lasted only days in use. Drivers did not want passengers at the platform end, both irate and late, to know their names! And how would you explain the state of this loco? J.L. Stevenson, courtesy Hamish Stevenson.**

73014 at Willesden on 9 May 1964 proving that even late in the day they could muster some respectability. There even seems to be a trace of yellow on the tender axleboxes; a near miracle, but then it is a few weeks out of works. This of course is the green apparition; once a Willesden engine but now working from Bletchley. Stephen Gradidge.

The End. Or one of the Ends anyway. Basingstoke shed on Saturday evening 7 July 1967, BR Class 5s cooling down for the last time; 73065 and 'decorated' 73093, with a Class 4 behind. Rod Hoyle.

73057 comes south past Kingmoor shed about 1956. Paul Chancellor Collection.

Concerning Tables

Compilation began with Southern Region Form BR9637: *Return of Locomotives undergoing or awaiting repairs at...* Thus the BR5s based on the SR on average carry more information in the tables including the mileage figures. Right at the end of steam maintenance at Eastleigh works 'foreign' subjects were noted 'MR.Loco'. or 'WR.Loco'. The BR9215 forms held at Kew, the 'Engine Record Cards' proved useful though they are not complete. The ERO 3666 'Engine History Cards' at the NRM are not complete either and there is in fact very little information for some of the engines. Finally, added into the mix, were the BR9221 forms, the 'Boiler Record Cards' held at York. Again, they are incomplete. At least two locomotives (73122 and 73152) have two (!) existing BR9215 cards on which a number of dates do not agree.

Mileages
The ERO 3666 forms recorded the annual mileage for what it is worth (the figures tend to be understated) for a number of years but not for all of the class; the BR9637 forms show the mileage since the previous General Overhaul. But no locomotive has a final mileage as annual mileage recording fell by the wayside in the early 1960s and the BR9637 forms 'mileage recordings of steam locomotives' were discontinued w/e 21/3/64.

Shed Allocations
Are as accurate as records allow and are all dated period ending. Boiler and tender information comes from the sources already mentioned but again are not complete.

Overhauls
These are classified in The Record as in most of 'The Book of...' series normally following the dates and in bold.
GO General Overhaul
HI Heavy Intermediate
HC Heavy Casual
LI Light Intermediate
LC Light Classified
NC Non-Classified
Some are followed by **[EO]** or **[TO]** which seems to mean Engine Only or Tender Only whilst **Rect.** means 'rectification'. **Adj** = Adjustment which is the same, more or less as **Rect**. AWS is often shown as ATC in the record.

Work carried out
Normally listed on the ERO 3666 cards and the BR 9637 forms, though a good number are listed on the back of the BR9215 forms but normally without any dates which is very frustrating. For the SR forms (BR9637) these were normally listed as Tests but were sometimes listed without numbers and in some cases these lists have been left intact. Examples include:
3329 Modified pistons for continuous blowdown valves
3345 Atomiser and bogie lubrication
3400 Manganese liners to Intermediate rubbing plates and buffer faces
3622 Alteration to spring balancing arrangement and fitting stops to prevent reversing gear jamming.
4983 BR type ATC equipment
5548 Hinged cab windows
5900 Safety links between engine and tender
3980 and 4175 Both fitting of padded back to fireman's seat
4175 Also referred to cab draught shield
It is amusing to reflect that ERO actually stands for E.R. O'Neil, an American citizen enlisted by Stamp to rationalise the LMS printing arrangements and streamline its multitude of pre-Group forms, procedures and so on. He set up a print works at Crewe in Wistaston Road and a whole series of standard forms were issued, classified EROxxxx etc. The Stationary Store at Crewe was always known as 'The ERO'!

Southern Region 'Tests'
T2081 Regulator valves and various boiler valves modified
T2238 Boiler fusible plug system modified
T2263 Piston rod modified packing
T2272 Piston head modification
T2278 Modified steam brake pipes
T2291 Modification of tender coal hole door plates for improved access
T2303 Improved axlebox grease lubrication

73088 at Eastleigh, 25 June 1960; it has yet to receive its JOYOUS GARD plates. 5P 5F above cab number. Bolted to the valence, they made little or no impact. A waste of time, was a common verdict. Stephen Gradidge.

The Book of the BR Standard Class 5 4-6-0s

The Record

73000

To traffic 12/4/51

Works
13/4/51-24/4/51	Derby Painting
26/6/51-2/7/51**NC**	8,880 Derby Driving gear
4/10/51-19/10/51**LC**	23,400 Derby P & V liners
22/4/52-20/5/52**LC**	52,794 Derby Cylinders
15/12/52-17/12/52**NC[EO]**	79,527 Derby
3/8/53-10/9/53**LI**	101,213 Derby R3622 Alterations to Spring balancing arrangement and fitting stops to prevent reversing gear jamming
20/5/54-17/6/54**LI**	29,098 Derby
13/9/54-21/10/54**LC**	39,165 Derby
15/10/56-16/11/56**GO**	105,067 Derby R3698 Provide and fitting new holding down bracket and packings R5900 Safety links between engine and tender
2/12/57-3/1/58**LC**	44,810 Derby E3329 Modified Pistons for continuous Blowdown valves
9/12/58-22/1/59**HI**	81,826 Doncaster
11/9/61-29/12/61**GO**	181,060 Doncaster
16/6/65-6/9/65**LI**	Cowlairs

Boilers
No.836 from new
No.859 16/11/56
No.849 29/12/61

Tender
BR1 type No.794 from new

Annual mileage
1951 36,440*
1952 44,227*
1953 33,732
1954 32,906
1955 34,183
1956 29,027
1957 40,575
*Includes mileage while o/l to other regions

Sheds
Perth 12/4/51*
Derby 16/6/51
Stratford 22/12//51
Derby 22/3/52
Millhouses 24/1/53
Derby 28/2/53
Nottingham 3/10/53
Grimesthorpe 10/5/58
Canklow 7/1/61
Derby 6/1/62
Woodford Halse 21/9/62
Oxley 16/1/65
Shrewsbury 3/4/65
Agecroft 30/4/66
Patricroft 22/10/66
*'Paper' transfer

Withdrawn week ending 30/3/68

73000 at Crewe on 5 May 1951, wearing its Derby 17A shedplate. Less than a fortnight before it had been at Marylebone for official examination by the board of the British Transport Executive. Unexpectedly, it transferred to Stratford on the Great Eastern Section at the end of the year and worked from there for about three months. It was a temporary transfer, made necessary by a shortage of new Britannias, suffering their axle problems. J.C. Flemons, www.transporttreasury.co.uk

It's not the most technically perfect picture you'll ever see but this is 73000 in its first moments, trundling up and down the works yard at Derby in its initial coat of grey paint with no cabside number, 12 April 1951. R.J. Buckley, Initial Photographics.

73000, with Derby 17A shedplate, on its first revenue-earning trip, at Derby station waiting to depart to Manchester. R.J. Buckley, Initial Photographics.

73001

To traffic 9/5/51

Works
18/7/51-21/7/51**NC**	786 Derby Draw gear
4/9/51-27/9/51**LC[EO]**	13,176 Derby Valves
15/11/51-13/12/51**LC[EO]**	8,841 Derby P & V liners
14/2/52-11/3/52**LC[EO]**	24,468 Derby P & V
19/12/52-12/1/53**LC[EO]**	58,817 Derby
7/9/53-1/10/53**LI**	85,717 Derby
	R3345 Atomiser and bogie lubrications
	R3400 Manganese liners to intermediate rubbing plates and intermediate buffer faces
	R3622 Modifications to reversing gear
	4175 Fitting padded back to fireman's seat
20/10/55-25/11/55**GO**	83,963 Derby
30/8/56-6/9/56**NC**	28,368 Derby
	ATC gear [WR type]
2/8/58-19/11/58**HI**	Swindon BR Green livery
24/11/59-8/3/60**NC**	Swindon
8/6/4-29/7/64**LC**	Eastleigh WR Loco

Boilers
No.837 from new
No.846 8/11/55

Tenders
BR1 No.795 from new
BR1 No.821 date unknown

Annual mileage
1951 20,167
1952 38,450
1953 37,910
1954 42,529
1955 34,829

Sheds
Deby 19/5/51
Salop 24/3/56
Swindon 1/12/56
Bristol Barrow Road 25/1/64
Gloucester Horton Road 7/2/65
Bath Green Park 7/3/65

Withdrawn 31/12/65

73001 new, lubricator still hidden, fresh out of works at Derby on 8 May 1951. In *The Stanier 4-6-0s of the LMS* (D&C, 1977) J.W.P. Rowledge and Brian Reed point out that all the effort to reduce preparation time was to some extent wasted, because under agreements of the period the time allowed a driver was based on the heating surface of the locomotive, with the dividing line set at 1,500sq. ft.. So it came to pass that *less* time was allowed for say, a Midland three cylinder Compound with three drive lines, six inside eccentrics and any number of inaccessible other parts than for a new BR Class 5 specially designed with economy of preparation time in mind. R.J. Buckley, Initial Photographics.

73002

To traffic 18/5/51

Works
4/6/51-5/6/51**LC**	2,182 Derby
20/7/51-26/7/51**NC**	8,775 Derby
17/9/51-6/10/51**LC**	16,696 Derby
1/1/53-29/1/53**LI**	71,009 Derby
4/2/53-17/2/53**LC**	102 Derby
19/2/53-24/2/53**NC[Rect]**	132 Derby
	4175 Fitting of cab draught shields
28/1/55-1/3/55**LI**	65,679 Derby
8/5/56-15/6/56**GO**	49,384 Derby
	R3698 Provide and fit new holding down bracket and packing
1/3/57-11/4/57**LC**	34,974 Derby
	E3329 Modified pistons for continuous blowdown valves
28/1/58-20/2/58**HI**	69,058 Derby
	R5900 Provide and fit safety links between engine and tender
	R6132 Fit protection shields
	R3400 Manganese liners – Buffer facers for intermediate rubbing plates
	55 copper stays riveted over 502 nuts renewed
8/8/60-17/9/60**GO**	Doncaster
10/1/63-9/2/63**LI**	Eastleigh
	2 SR type fusible plugs; Blowdown operating gear; Briquette tube feeder; Draught screens; Tender coalhole door plates; Grease lubrication to axlebox and spring buckle pins; Steam brake isolating cock; Speedometer; 515 monel metal stays riveted over 515 nuts renewed 151 new small tubes 'Stewart and Lloyds'
26/2/64-7/3/64**NC**	102,352 Eastleigh E4983 ATC
12/8/65-15/9/65**LC**	Eastleigh

Boilers
No.838 from new
No.839 15/6/56
No.1505 17/9/60

Tender
BR1 no.796 from new

Annual mileage
1951 32,428*
1952 38,581
1953 32,856
1954 30,548
1955 36,428
1956 41,664
1957 41,050
*Includes mileage whilst o/l to another Region

Sheds
Derby 19/5/51
Stratford 22/11/51
Derby 31/12/51
Nottingham 3/10/53
Canklow 10/5/58
Millhouses 9/1/60
Canklow 29/4/61
Eastleigh 17/12/62
Weymouth 16/9/63

Withdrawn 1/66

73002 at Bristol Barrow Road shed, 15 July 1956. This one too was sent to Stratford at the end of 1951 to cover for errant Britannias though it seems to have spent little more than the festive season there. It transferred to Eastleigh from the LMR in 1962 and ended up at Weymouth so it worked from sheds of LMS, LNER, SR and GWR origin. H.C. Casserley, courtesy R.M. Casserley.

73003 at Kentish Town shed, 17 July 1955. The smokebox door lamp iron is a feature which did not become general until the 1960s, when they were moved because of the risk from overhead cables. This one was fitted when 73003, 73015 and 73017 were loaned to Nine Elms in 1953, when the engines needed to display the Bournemouth line headcode.

73003

No engine record card held at the National Archive

To traffic 31/5/51

Works
21/8/51-1/9/51**LC**	11,524	Derby
18/2/52-8/3/52**LC**	29,029	Derby
10/6/52-5/8/52**LC**	42,287	Derby
23/11/53-31/12/53**HI**	96,565	Derby

5/4175 Cab draught shields and padded back to fireman's seat
R3400 Manganes liners buffer faces
R3345 Atomiser and bogie lubrication
R3622 Alterations to spring balancing arrangement and fitting stops to prevent reversing gear jamming. 207 nuts renewed 5 brick arch studs

10/2/54-31/3/54**LC**	2,427	Derby
1/2/56-27/3/56**GO**	75,653	Derby

R3698 Provide and fit new holding down bracket and packing

8/6/56-14/6/56**LC[EO]**	13,205	Derby

P/E 16/6/57 E3329 Modified pistons for continuous blowdown valve

4/1/58-30/1/58**HI**	79,470	Derby

R5900 Safety links between engine and tender
R6132 Protecting shield over leading axle

11/59 Swindon BR green livery

Boilers
No.839 from new
No.1617 27/3/56
No.1003 11/1/62

Tender
BR1 no.797 from new

Annual mileage
1951 23,974
1952 36,882
1953 35,709
1954 35,480
1955 36,211
1956 41,056
1957 42,347

Sheds
Leicester Midland 16/6/51
Bristol Barrow Road 25/1/58
Shrewsbury 30/3/63
Bristol Barrow Road 28/9/63
Oxford 11/7/65

Withdrawn 2/65

73003, ex-works at Derby on 27 March 1956; 'flexible screens' prominent. It had been involved in a collision at New Street early in 1954, bringing about the demise of Compound 41047. Its 'Bournemouth line' smokebox door lamp iron has survived the visit to Derby. Peter Groom.

73004

To traffic 8/6/51

Works
31/8/51-12/9/51**LC**	10,860 Derby V and P Draw gear
5/12/52-13/12/52**NC[EO]**	65,047 Derby Reversing gear
27/10/53-26/11/53**LI**	91,879 Derby R3400 Manganese liners to intermediate rubbing plates and buffer faces.
	R3622 Alteration to spring balancing arrangement and fitting stops to prevent reversing gear jamming
	4175 Cab draught shields and padded back to fireman's seat
	R3345 Atomiser and bogie lubrication
	330 nuts renewed 4 brick arch studs
20/2/56-12/4/56**GO**	85,817 Derby
	R3698 New holding down bracket and packing
	P/e 16/6/57 E3329 Modified pistons for continuous blowdown valves
15/10/58-26/11/58**HI**	Doncaster
24/3/60-21/4/60**LC[EO]**	63,181 Derby Timken bearing
19/9/61-27/10/61**GO**	109,361 Cowlairs
16/4/64-5/6/64**HC**	Darlington
27/7/64-12/9/64**LC**	Darlington

Sheds
Leicester Midland 16/6/51
Derby 22/12/51
Leicester Midland 31/12/51
Heaton Mersey 26/2/57
Leicester Midland 23/3/57
Millhouses 10/5/58
Chester Midland 6/2/60
Willesden 14/5/60
Bletchley 7/3/64
Nuneaton 9/1/65
Croes Newydd 19/6/65
Bolton 30/4/66

Boilers
No.840 from new
No.1618 12/4/56
No.1635 27/10/61

Tenders
BR1 no.798 from new
BR1 no.808

Withdrawn 10/67

73004, a few weeks old, at Burton on Trent on 17 July 1951. Its first layer of grime is well on the way. R.J. Buckley, Initial Photographics.

73005

To traffic 20/6/51

Works
2/7/51-6/7/51**NC**	Derby
4/5/53-29/5/53**LI**	St. Rollox
15/2/54-27/2/54**LC[EO]**	St. Rollox
27/7/54-7/8/54**LC[EO]**	St. Rollox
8/11/54**NC**	St. Rollox
4/1/55-29/1/55**LI**	St. Rollox
24/3/55-7/4/55**LC[EO]**	Shed
4/7/55-12/7/55**NC[EO]**	St. Rollox
15/5/55-28/5/55**NC[EO]**	St. Rollox
29/8/55-23/9/55**HC[EO]**	St. Rollox
23/12/55-30/12/55**HC[EO]**	St. Rollox
25/1/56-18/2/56**GO**	St. Rollox
19/3/56-24/3/56**NC[EO]**	St. Rollox
23/4/56-3/5/56**NC[EO]**	St. Rollox
11/3/57-16/3/57**LC[EO]**	St. Rollox
17/5/57-27/6/57**HI**	St. Rollox
28/10/57-31/10/57**LC[EO]**	St. Rollox
5/5/58-7/6/58**LC[TO]**	Cowlairs
24/1/59-14/2/59**LI**	Cowlairs
5/3/59-7/3/59**NC[EO]**	Cowlairs
22/2/60-12/3/60**LC**	Cowlairs
11/5/60-28/6/60**NC[EO]**	Cowlairs
9/8/60-2/9/60**NC**	Cowlairs
18/10/60-4/11/60**NC[EO]**	Cowlairs
27/1/61-25/2/61**LC[EO]**	Cowlairs
21/8/61-7/10/61**GO**	Cowlairs
24/4/63-25/5/63**HI**	Cowlairs
3/1/64-4/2/64**LC[TO]**	Cowlairs

Boiler
No.841 from new

Tenders
BR1 no.799 from new
BR1 no.801
BR1 no.786

Sheds
Perth 23/8/51
Corkerhill 19/1/63

Withdrawn 27/6/66

73005 at St Rollox, 11 September 1955. At the left-hand edge of the smokebox rim is a valve to which could be attached a steam lance for clearing the boiler tubes. It is fed (from the header) through a valve near the chimney. Thin piping off this serves the whistle (operated by a wire running through the handrail). A further pipe run disappears behind the running plate to deliver atomised steam to the lubricators just behind the steam pipe. H.C. Casserley, courtesy R.M. Casserley.

On 12 April 1954 snowplough-fitted 73005 has the Granite City at the granite city, Aberdeen. It had arrived from its birthplace, Derby, back in 1951 on 10 July, with the 11.30 am Carlisle-Perth parcels and within a couple of days had been hard at it on two return trips a day, to Buchanan Street and to Carstairs. J. Robertson, www.transporttreasury.co.uk

73006

To traffic 28/6/51

Works
5/7/51-11/7/51**NC**	Derby
12/6/52-26/6/52**LC**	St. Rollox
9/6/53-27/6/53**LI**	St. Rollox
6/4/54-23/4/54**LC[EO]**	St. Rollox
2/11/54-26/11/54**LI**	St. Rollox
13/1/55-20/1/55**NC[EO]**	St. Rollox
1/2/55-12/2/55**LC[EO]**	St. Rollox
15/11/55-24/11/55**LC**	St. Rollox
7/2/56-9/2/56**NC[EO]**	St. Rollox
23/4/56-25/5/56**GO**	St. Rollox
10/10/57-14/11/57**HI**	St. Rollox
28/10/58-8/11/58**LC[EO]**	St. Rollox
21/4/59-9/5/59**HI**	Cowlairs
20/5/59-21/5/59**Return**	Cowlairs
14/10/60-18/10/60**LC[EO]**	Cowlairs
14/2/61-18/3/61**GO**	Cowlairs
24/10/61-25/10/61**LC[EO]**	Cowlairs
5/12/62-15/12/62**LC**	Cowlairs
12/9/63-20/9/63**LC**	Cowlairs
31/1/64-6/2/64**NC[EO]**	Cowlairs
8/9/64-29/10/64**LI**	Eastleigh MR loco.

Boiler
No.842 from new

Tender
BR1 no.800 from new

Sheds
Perth 23/6/51
Corkerhill 19/1/63
Patricroft 18/7/64

Withdrawn 11/3/67

A beautifully lined black 73006, more or less new by the look of it, with the Saint Mungo at Stirling. It was one of a batch of five, 73005-73009 which had gone new to Perth, even though nowhere on earth was already so well-provided for with respect to Class 5 power. There were misgivings about the new Standards on the Scottish Region (see *A Mixed Reception?* for instance) but they were put on some of the best trains, working turn and turn about with Black Fives at the better end of the maintenance cycle. M. Robertson, www.transporttreasury.co.uk

73007

To traffic 9/7/51

Works
25/9/51-4/10/51**LC[EO]**	St. Rollox
7/4/52-29/4/52**LC[EO]**	St. Rollox
10/8/53-5/9/53**LI**	St. Rollox
27/1/54-13/2/54**LC[EO]**	St. Rollox
15/2/54-17/2/54**NC[EO]**	St. Rollox
20/3/54-16/4/54**LC[EO]**	St. Rollox
9/11/54-10/11/54**NC[EO]**	St. Rollox
11/5/55-4/6/55**GO**	St. Rollox
16/6/55-25/6/55**NC[EO]**	St. Rollox
9/4/56-14/5/56**LC**	Crewe
4/9/56-13/9/56**NC[EO]**	St. Rollox
17/12/56-26/1/57**HI**	St. Rollox
30/5/57-6/6/57**NC[EO]**	St. Rollox
30/10/57-2/11/57**LC[EO]**	St. Rollox
5/12/57-13/12/57**NC[EO]**	St. Rollox
26/5/58-21/6/58**HI**	Cowlairs
2/7/58-17/7/58**LC[EO]**	Cowlairs
24/12/59-5/3/60**GO**	Cowlairs
15/8/60-17/9/60**LC[EO]**	Cowlairs
22/11/61-2/12/61**LC**	Cowlairs
25/4/62-9/6/62**HI**	Cowlairs
3/6/63-22/6/63**LC[EO]**	Cowlairs
16/4/64-30/5/64**LI**	Cowlairs
11/5/65-15/5/65**NC**	Cowlairs
20/10/65-23/10/65**NC[EO]**	Cowlairs
21/12/65-31/12/65**NC**	Cowlairs

Boiler
No.843 from new

Tenders
BR1 no.801 from new
BR1 no.799
BR1B no.1304
BR1 no.799

Sheds
Perth 9/7/51
Grangemouth 25/7/64
Stirling 30/10/65

Withdrawn 3/3/66

Snowplough-fitted (in June!) 73007, another of the Perth batch, arriving at Aberdeen on 22 June 1953. R. Butterfield, Initial Photographics.

73007 with the 7.0pm for Inverness, leaving Aviemore on 6 August 1953.
J.L. Stevenson, courtesy Hamish Stevenson.

73007 on the 5.30pm Glasgow train, at Aberdeen on 5 June 1964; the burnished disc on the smokebox door was one of a variety of pleasing Scottish Region touches. J.L. Stevenson, courtesy Hamish Stevenson.

Waiting for the Saint Mungo at Perth, 17 September 1954. The heavy iron brackets hanging under the buffer beam carried the snowplough; the holes drilled at the lower edge were for bolts that were part of the fixing too. At this period the Saint Mungo, the 5.30pm from Glasgow Buchanan Street, was re-engined at Perth. 73007 is waiting in one of the bays at the north end, with a Black Five and coaches behind. J.L. Stevenson, courtesy Hamish Stevenson.

On the appearance of the BR Class 5s at Perth in 1951 *The Railway Observer* commented that the crews were not particularly impressed and that the new engines lacked something 'when it came to hill climbing'. They would struggle on the Highland section, it was thought. The first one to get to Inverness was 73007, piloting a Black Five in July 1951. Whether it struggled or not is not recorded but it was back there in August, as we saw earlier; here it is on the Inverness turntable on 16 April 1957. The engine carries the G&SW Manson type tablet catching apparatus on the cabside. J.L. Stevenson, courtesy Hamish Stevenson.

73008

To traffic 13/7/51

Works
23/5/52-28/5/52**NC**	Derby
26/9/53-17/10/53**LI**	St. Rollox
15/12/53-9/1/54**LC[EO]**	St. Rollox
16/11/54**NC[EO]**	St. Rollox
8/3/55-9/4/55**GO**	St. Rollox
14/4/55-16/4/55**NC[EO]**	St. Rollox
27/2/56-29/2/56**NC**	St. Rollox
28/4/56-2/6/56**HI**	St. Rollox
3/9/56-13/10/56**HC[EO]**	St. Rollox
5/11/56-16/11/56 **HC[EO]**	St. Rollox
20/11/56-1/12/56**LC[EO]**	St. Rollox
2/8/57-6/9/57**LC[EO]**	St. Rollox
26/9/57-26/10/57**LC[EO]**	St. Rollox
28/11/57-21/12/57**HI**	St. Rollox
11/10/58-25/10/58**HC**	Cowlairs
28/11/58-24/12/58**LC[EO]**	Cowlairs
20/5/59-13/6/59**GO**	Cowlairs
2/11/60-10/12/60**LI**	Cowlairs
27/3/61-20/4/61**LC[EO]**	Cowlairs
20/9/61-14/10/61**LC[EO]**	Cowlairs
3/8/62-8/9/62**HI**	Cowlairs
5/11/62-14/1/62**NC[EO]**	Cowlairs
20/5/63-13/6/63**LC[EO]**	Cowlairs
28/5/64-27/6/64**LC[EO]**	Cowlairs

Boiler
No.844 from new

Tender
BR1 no.802 from new

Sheds
Perth 14/7/51
Rugby Testing Plant 8/9/51
Perth 22/3/52
Aberdeen Ferryhill 3/8/64

Withdrawn 20/9/65

73009

To traffic 19/7/51

Works
30/7/51-3/8/51**NC**	Crewe
11/4/53-30/4/53**LI**	St. Rollox
7/7/53-17/7/53**LC[EO]**	St. Rollox
13/9/54-16/10/54**LI**	St. Rollox
18/11/54**NC[EO]**	St. Rollox
2/2/55-4/3/55**LC[EO]**	St. Rollox
28/3/55-7/4/55**NC[EO]**	St. Rollox
28/4/55-30/4/55**NC[EO]**	St. Rollox
31/12/55-12/1/56**NC[EO]**	St. Rollox
29/2/56-1/3/56**NC**	St. Rollox
5/3/56-20/4/56**GO**	St. Rollox
9/6/56-30/8/56**HC[EO]**	St. Rollox
21/12/57-20/2/58**HI**	St. Rollox
12/9/59-10/10/59**LI**	Cowlairs
19/9/60-8/10/60**LC[EO]**	Cowlairs
20/6/61-30/6/61**NC[EO]**	Cowlairs
28/12/61-10/2/62**GO**	Cowlairs
22/9/64-14/11/64**LI**	Darlington
16/11/64-25/11/64**NC**	Darlington
6/8/65-14/8/65**NC[EO]**	Cowlairs

Sheds
Perth 19/7/51
Corkerhill 19/1/63

Boiler
No.845 from new

Tender
BR1 no.803 from new

Withdrawn 14/7/66

73009 on the 7.5pm to Inverness (via Forres) leaving Aviemore on 12 August 1952; Highland section tablet catching apparatus on the cabside. J.L. Stevenson, courtesy Hamish Stevenson.

73010

To traffic 14/8/51

Works

2/1/53-8/1/53**NC[EO]**	67,068 Derby Modifications
10/8/53-2/9/53**LI**	89,061 Derby
	R3345 Atomiser and bogie lubrication
	R3400 Manganese liners to intermediate rubbing plates and buffer faces
	R3622 Alterations to spring balancing arrangement and fitting stops to prevent reversing gear jamming
	4175 Cab draught shields and padded back to fireman's seat
23/5/55-7/7/55**GO**	77,531 Derby
25/9/56-24/10/56**HI**	54,335 Derby
	P/E 16/6/57 E3329 Modified pistons for continuous blowdown valves
6/1/58-10/1/58**NC**	Doncaster
31/5/58-14/6/58**LC**	111,587 Doncaster
7/7/59-13/8/59**HI**	114,997 Doncaster
2/5/60-8/6/60**LC**	38,576 Derby
30/8/61-19/10/61**GO**	82,003 Derby
	E5173 Fitting of Speed indicators
	E4341 Downs sanding gear removed
	R5900 Safety links between engine and tender
11/5/65-29/5/65**LI**	Cowlairs

Annual Mileage
1951 9,052
1952 48,016
1953 39,424
1954 44,658
1955 41,855
1956 36,795
1957 41,751
1958 34,432
1959 50,805
1960 43,007

Sheds
Leeds Holbeck 18/8/51
Leicester Central 8/9/59
Neasden 13/6/60
Woodford Halse 30/6/62
Oxley 16/1/65
Patricroft 28/3/65

Boilers
No.846 from new
No.1498 7/7/55
No.1757 19/10/61

Tender
BR1 no.804 from new

Withdrawn 22/6/68

Shiny new 73010 in Derby shed yard, 16 August 1951. R.J. Buckley, Initial Photographics.

73011

To traffic 17/8/51

Works
21/1/53-28/1/53**NC[EO]**	76,407 Derby Modifications
7/4/53-23/4/53**LC**	81,715 Derby P and V liners
	4175 Cab draught shields
23/8/54-23/9/54**LI**	34,469 Derby
10/11/54-25/11/54**LC[EO]**	4,286 Derby
	R3400 Manganes liners to rubbing plates and buffer faces
	R3345 Atomiser and bogie lubrication
	R3622 Alterations to Spring balancing arrangement and fitting stops to prevent reversing gear jamming
24/9/56-26/10/56**GO**	71,105 Derby
	E3329 Modified pistons for continuous blowdown valves
1/10/58-14/11/58**GO**	Doncaster
25/4/61-30/5/61**HI**	96,189 Derby
	E4983 AWS equipment
	E5173 Speed indicator and recorder
5/11/62-7/12/62**GO**	Derby
	R6132 Protection shield
15/9/64-16/10/64**LC**	Eastleigh MR loco

Annual Mileage
1951 20,885
1952 53,650
1953 39,324
1954 27,199
1955 39,534
1956 33,726
1957 47,686
1958 37,820
1959 50,070
1960 34,105
Mileage at 2/1/60: 324,625

Boilers
No.847 from new
No.850 26/20/56
No.1911 16/10/64

Tender
BR1 no.805 from new

Sheds
Leeds Holbeck 18/8/51
Sheffield [Millhouses] 14/9/53
Holyhead 31/1/60
Llandudno Jct. 9/2/63
Woodford Halse 2/11/63
Oxley 16/1/65
Patricroft 3/4/65

Withdrawn 11/11/67

73012

To traffic 24/8/51

Works
1/9/51-5/9/51**LC[EO]**	64 Derby
	Piston and oiling test
2/2/53-11/2/53**NC[EO]**	63,357 Derby
	4175 Cab draught shields and fitting padded back to fireman's seat
18/8/54-16/9/54**LI-HI**	105,743 Derby
	R3345 Atomiser and bogie lubrication
	R3622 Alterations to spring balancing arrangement and fitting stops to prevent reversing gear jamming
19/3/56-26/4/56**GO**	58,620 Derby
	R3698 Provide and fit new holding down bracket and packing
	R3400 Manganese liners to intermediate rubbing plates and buffer faces
	R4542 Additional cross bracing to frame
	ATC equipment [WR type]
26/8/58-2/12/58**HI**	Swindon BR Green Livery
2/10/59-24/12/59**LC**	Swindon

Annual mileage
1951 19,344
1952 42,304
1953 33,422
1954 953*
1955 37,485*
Miles run whilst on loan to other regions

Boilers
No.848 from new
No.856 26/4/56

Tender
BR1 no.806 from new

Sheds
Leeds 25/8/51
Millhouses 14/9/53
Shrewsbury 21/9/53
Swindon 1/12/56
Bristol Barrow Road 22/6/64

Withdrawn 12/64

The sun glints off 73012, fresh off Derby works after a Light Intermediate (a glance at the table shows the precise dates do not match – this was common) and ready for the trip home to Shrewsbury, 17 September 1954. R.J. Buckley, Initial Photographics.

The 4.0pm for Hereford at Birmingham Snow Hill, with 73012 in charge, 3 August 1957. The strange apparatus on smokebox side is the WR ATC brake valve, to shut off steam to the ejector. The gent on the platform is singularly unimpressed; was he a Castle devotee? Michael Mensing.

73013

To traffic 31/8/51

Works
11/5/53-27/5/53**LC**	72,780 Derby
	PV liners
	4175 Cab draught shields and Padded back to fireman's seat
	R3622 Alterations to spring balancing arrangement and fitting stops to prevent reversing gear jamming
8/10/54-13/11/54**LI**	124,672 Horwich
30/5/56-29/6/56**GO**	52,209 Derby
	R3698 Modifications to tank holding down bracket
	R3345 Atomiser and bogie lubrication
	ATC equipment [WR type]
5/5/58-5/6/58**HI**	56,092 Derby
	MDL/1346 Tender axles treated with zinc rich primer and black enamel to reduce corrosion
17/3/59-9/4/59**LC**	26,283 Derby
25/11/59-21/12/59**LC**	47,780 Derby
19/9/60-18/10/60**LI**	70,423 Derby
	R3400 Manganese liners to intermediate rubbing plates and buffer faces
24/8/62-20/9/62**GO**	Derby
	E4983 ATC equipment
11/2/63-7/3/63**LC**	Derby

Annual mileage
1951 20,036
1952 42,100
1953 35,520
1954 31,531*
1955 35,175*
1956 30,790
1957 28,265
1958 29,892
1959 28,179
1960 30,385
*Miles run whilst on loan to other regions

Boilers
No.850 from new
No.848 19/6/56

Tender
BR1 no.807 from new

Sheds
Millhouses 1/9/51
Shrewsbury 19/9/53
Chester West 16/7/55
Chester Midland 26/9/59
Willesden 14/5/60
Bletchley 7/3/64
Oxley 16/1/65
Banbury 19/6/65
Bolton 30/4/66

Withdrawn 7/5/66

73013 at its Willesden home, 19 May 1963. Subtly different pattern of electrification flashes from 73016 at Eastleigh, say. Speedometer fitted by now, yellow tender axleboxes, lamp iron rearranged on smokebox door. Stephen Gradidge.

73014

To traffic 6/9/51

Works
27/2/52-20/3/52**LI**	20,558 Derby PV Liners
9/3/53-7/4/53**LC**	62,507 Derby
4/8/53-31/8/53**LC**	73,389 Derby
	R3622 Alterations to spring balancing arrangement and fitting stops to prevent reversing gear jamming
	4175 Cab draught shields and fitting padded back to fireman's seat
25/10/54-25/11/54**LI**	113,225 Derby
	R3345 Atomiser and bogie lubrication
	R3400 Manganese liners to intermediate rubbing plates and buffer faces
	402 nuts renewed 4 brick arch studs
26/4/56-14/5/56**LC**	48,918 Derby
	ATC equipment [WR type]
28/5/57-5/7/57**GO**	90,495 Derby
	E3329 Modified pistons for continuous blowdown valves
	R5900 Safety links between engine and tender
5/8/59-31/8/59**LC**	71,646 Derby
20/6/60-8/7/60**HI**	92,097 Derby
	E5173 Speed indicator and recorder
16/3/61-13/4/61**HI**	29,311 Derby
	E4983 ATC equipment
9/6/61-23/6/61**NC**	33,625 Derby
15/1/63-12/2/63**LC**	Derby
30/1/64-14/3/64**GO**	Eastleigh MR loco BR Green livery
	Insert patches to flanges of copper tube back plate nitro arc welded

Annual mileage
1951 16,267
1952 39,901
1953 26,174
1954 34,970*
1955 31,758*
1956 39,184
1957 41,231
1958 26,902
1959 28,750
1960 31,965
*Miles run whilst on loan to other regions

Boilers
No.853 from new
No.855 5/7/57
No.1631 14/3/64

Tenders
BR1 no.808 from new
BR1 no.798

Sheds
Millhouses 8/9/51
WR O/L 19/9/53
Shrewsbury 3/10/53
Cardiff Canton 13/8/55
Chester West 2/9/58
Chester Midland 9/4/60
Willesden 14/5/60
Bletchley 7/3/64
Oxley 16/1/65
Banbury 19/6/65
Bolton 30/4/66

Withdrawn 22/7/67

On that familiar spot outside the Derby roundhouse, on 5 July 1957 and another Western Region Class 5, Canton's 73014 with new second emblem, is readied to go home after overhaul. The coat of Eastleigh green is still some years away. R.J. Buckley, Initial Photographics.

73014 in later life, well-plastered with OHL warnings, under the wires at what looks like Stockport. Paul Chancellor Collection.

73015

To traffic 12/9/51

Works
11/8/52-2/9/52**LC**	37,118 Derby
5/12/52-29/12/52**LC[EO]**	47,103 Derby PV liners
10/2/53-4/3/53**LC**	51,680 Derby PV liners
13/8/53-8/9/53**LC**	70,444 Derby
	4175 Cab draught shields and padded back to fireman's seat
	R3622 Alterations to spring balancing arrangement and fittings stops to prevent reversing gear jamming PV liners
25/10/54-19/11/54**LI**	113,911 Derby
	R3345 Atomiser and bogie lubrication
	R3400 Manganese liners to intermediate rubbing plates and buffer faces
7/2/55-22/2/55**LC**	7,889 Derby
9/2/56-16/3/56**GO**	45,999 Derby
1/10/56-1/11/56**LC[EO]**	80,286 Derby
	E3329 Modified pistons for continuous blowdown valves
12/9/57-7/10/57**HI**	Derby
	R5900 Safety links fitted between engine and tender
20/7/59-1/1/60**GO**	Swindon BR Green Livery

Annual mileage
1951 16,741
1952 30,426
1953 35,812
1954 36,145*
1955 37,496
1956 35,953
1957 43,468
*Miles run whilst on loan to other regions

Boilers
No.856 from new
No.837 16/3/56
No.1996 19/5/62

Tender
BR1 no.809 from new

Sheds
Millhouses 15/9/51
Shrewsbury 14/9/53
Derby 5/3/56
Bristol Barrow Road 18/5/57
Bath Green Park 11/7/65

Withdrawn 8/65

73016

To traffic 21/9/51

Works
25/9/51-2/10/51**LC**	70 Derby
12/11/51-19/12/51**LC**	3,037 Derby
4/2/53-4/3/53**LC**	54,735 Derby
3/9/53-1/10/53**LC**	75,795 Derby
	R3622 Alterations to Spring balancing arrangement and fitting stops to prevent reversing gear jamming
	4175 Cab draught shield and padded back to fireman's seat
27/4/54-27/5/54**LI**	96,199 Derby
	R3400 Manganese liners to intermediate rubbing plates and buffer faces
	4 brick arch studs
24/1/55-10/2/55**LC**	29,592 Derby
	432 nuts renewed
28/2/56-10/3/56**LC**	71,116 Derby
14/5/56-7/6/56**LI**	75,593 Derby
	429 new nuts 12 brick arch studs
17/12/56-30/1/57**GO**	22,558 Derby
	R5900 Safety links between engine and tender
18/10/63-19/11/63**LC**	142,430 Eastleigh

Boilers
No.851 from new
No.861 30/1/57
No.1905 13/2/59

Tender
BR1 no.810 from new

Annual mileage
1951 3,710
1952 48,480
1953 33,752
1954 38,623
1955 39,812
1956 30,072
1957 42,912

Sheds
Grimesthorpe 6/10/51
Millhouses 23/2/52
Derby 24/1/53
Millhouses 21/3/53
Canklow 6/1/62
Eastleigh 17/12/62
Feltham 6/1/64
Nine Elms 20/11/64
Feltham 25/10/65
Weymouth 22/11/65

Withdrawn 1/67

73016 at Eastleigh shed in 1965. It has had some selective attention, to the cylinders obviously, and probably the smokebox and the motion. It certainly wasn't thought necessary to clean it! The running plate ahead of the cylinder has come off to get the piston and/or piston valve out, and the number has been chalked on to make sure it goes back on the right engine. The chime whistle has been replaced by a standard whistle behind the chimney – this occasionally happened. The electrification flashes have been wiped and show out clearly – it was widespread practice to clean them at say, X-day examinations. Nevertheless it's hard to imagine them saving many from electrocution; there was none of the impact, say, of the SNCF's cab notice *Attention – danger de mort!* with a lightening bolt and a stricken man! www.transporttreasury.co.uk

73017

[No card at the National Archive]

To traffic 28/9/51

Works
28/3/53-25/4/53**LC**   60,629 Shed
21/5/55-30/6/55**LI**   117,160 Derby
R3345 Atomiser and bogie lubrication
R3980 Cab draught shields and padded back to fireman's seat
R3400 Manganese liners to rubbing plates and buffer faces
21/6/56**NC**   37,852 Derby ATC gear [GWR type]
19/3/57-26/4/57**GO**   61,126 Derby 87 copper studs 12 brick arch studs 12 copper washers
10/9/59-26/9/59**LI**   73,711 Eastleigh 5548 Hinged cab windows
Piston rod packing blowdown gear injector overflow pipes
steam brake isolating cock
3/8/61-9/9/61**GO**   120,947 Eastleigh
Washout plugs and pipework
T2238 Fusible plugs and back plug SR type front plug BR type
T2291 Modification of tender coal hole doors plates for improved access

Annual Mileage
1951 10,855
1952 43,461
1953 23,738
1954 27,151*
1955 32,994*
*Miles run whilst o/l to other regions

Boilers
No.849 from new
No.858 26/4/57
No.1502 9/9/61

Tender
BR1 no.811 from new

Sheds
Nottingham 6/10/51
Shrewsbury 3/10/53
Cardiff Canton 16/6/56
Shrewsbury 14/7/56
Swindon 1/12/56
Weymouth 4/10/58

Withdrawn 10/64

73017 at Derby on 26 April 1957, newly steamed after its General. R.J. Buckley, Initial Photographics.

73018

To traffic 4/10/51

Works
15/6/53-4/7/53**LC**	59,745 Shed
18/10/54-17/11/54**HI**	102,919 Derby
17/4/56-21/5/56**GO**	52,667 Derby
11/3/58-24/4/58**LC**	
9/6/59-27/6/59**LI-HI**	85,070 Eastleigh Steam brake pipes Isolating cock Blowdown valve operating gear
	R5900 Fitting of safety links between engine and tender
	520 monel metal stays riveted over 520 nuts renewed
	151 new small tubes 'Stewart and Lloyds'
10/11/61-30/12/61**GO**	152,248 Eastleigh Green livery?
	W/E 9/12/61 awaiting boiler
	Boiler washout plugs and pipework
	5548 Provision and fitting of hinged cab windows Speedometer fitted
	5731 Modification of grease lubricator for axlebox and spring bracket pin
	T2291 Modification of tender coal hole door plates for improved access
	Modification of Briquette tube feeder
	2 fusible plugs patch fitted to Barrel plate
10/12/62-15/12/62**NC-LC**	30,997 Eastleigh

Annual mileage
1951 10,700
1952 37,771
1953 28,349
1954 30,361*
1955 40,495*
*Miles run whilst o/l to other regions

Boilers
No.853 from new
No.840 21/5/56
No.858 30/12/61

Tenders
BR1 no.812 from new
BR1 no.868 7/4/56 on Shrewsbury shed

Sheds
Nottingham 6/10/51
Shrewsbury 3/10/53
Swindon 1/12/56
Weymouth 4/10/58
Guildford 25/3/67

Withdrawn 7/67

73018 at Feltham shed, 8 January 1961; typically Southern absence of electrification flashes, no speedometer, short reach rod to lubricator. 73018 is said to have got green livery at Swindon in 1958 but there is no doubt about the date of this photograph, 1961; the lining shows it to be definitely in black. Perhaps the green came in the General at Eastleigh later in the year (see table above). Stephen Gradidge.

73019

To traffic 10/10/51

Works
30/9/52-22/10/52**LC**	41,552 Derby PV liners
7/12/54-4/1/55**LI**	92,201 Derby 474 nuts renewed
14/5/56-30/5/56**LC**	40,014 Derby ATC equipment [WR type]
18/2/56-25/1/57**GO**	59,865 Derby
3/3/58**NC**	Bristol
21/1/59-28/2/59**LI-HI**	54,379 Eastleigh
	W/E 21/2/59 awaiting wheels
	T2081 Regulator valves and various boiler valves modified- stainless steel
	240 monel metal stays riveted over 251 nuts renewed
	40 firehole rivets and 32 Foundation Ring rivets repaired
2/2/61-11/3/61**GO**	130,122 Eastleigh
	5548 Provision and fitting of hinged cab windows
	cab lifting brackets
25/11/63-4/1/64**LI**	80,220 Eastleigh WR loco
17/11/64-20/11/64**LC**	Eastleigh WR loco

Annual mileage
1951 7,919
1952 40,173
1953 24,651
1954 19,458*
1955 30,965
*Miles run whilst o/l to other regions

Boilers
No.854 from new
No.863 25/1/57
No.1495 11/3/61

Tenders
BR1 no.813 from new
BR1 no.816
BR1 no.813

Sheds
Nottingham 10/10/51
Bristol St. Philips Marsh 14/9/53
Bath Green Park 14/6/58
Bristol Barrow Road 16/7/60
Bath Green Park 8/10/60
Gloucester Barnwood 21/4/62
Gloucester Horton Road 4/5/64
Oxley 7/11/64
Bolton 30/4/66

Withdrawn 14/1/67

73020

[No card at the National Archive]

To traffic 16/10/51

Works
12/1/53-24/1/53**NC[EO]**	52,648 Crewe
10/4/53-11/5/53**LC**	57,373 Derby
6/10/55-3/11/55**LI**	116,777 Derby
	R3400 Manganese liners to intermediate rubbing plates and buffer faces
	R3345 Atomiser and bogie lubrication
30/7/56-6/6/56**NC[EO]**	22,210 Derby
6/9/56	Fitted with ATC equipment [WR type]
19/8/59-5/9/59**LI**	69,896 Eastleigh
	T2263 Injector overflow pipes Isolating cock blowdown gear
	5548 Fitting of hinged cab windows
	Seams and 76 studs repaired 2 fusible plugs
	580 monel metal stays riveted over 580 nuts renewed
13/10/61-25/11/61**GO**	194,482 Eastleigh
	Boiler washout plugs and pipework,
	T2291 Modification of tender coal hole door plates for improved access
	5731 Modification of grease lubricator for axlebox and spring bracket pin
	Modification of briquette tube feeder
	T2238 Modification of boiler fusible plug system, front plug SR, back plug BR

Annual Mileage
1951 9,574
1952 41,797
1953 24,520*
1954 27,074*
1955 17,809*
*Includes mileage run whilst on loan to other regions

Boilers
No.855 from new
No.854 6/3/57
No.1497 25/11/61

Tender
BR1 no.814 from new

Sheds
Chester Midland 3/11/51
Willesden 27/9/52
Chester Midland 18/10/52
Chester West 3/10/53
Shrewsbury 9/10/54
Swindon 1/12/56
Weymouth 13/10/58
Guildford 22/4/67

Withdrawn 7/7/67

73020 at Derby, newly emerged on 19 October 1951. R.J. Buckley, Initial Photographics.

A filthy black 73020, with standard whistle, at Southampton's Ocean terminal, waiting to leave with the Cunarder (chalked, deeply unimpressively on the smokebox) in the last weeks of Southern Region steam, on 21 June 1967. One of the Ruston and Hornsby diesel dock pilots stands on the left. Frank Sherlock.

73021

To traffic 22/10/51

Works
20/2/53-25/2/53**NC**	56,419 Crewe
17/9/53-15/10/53**LC**	78,731 Derby
	R3622 Alterations to Spring balancing arrangement and fitting stops to prevent reversing gear jamming
	4175 Cab draught shields and fitting padded back to fireman's seat
9/2/55-4/3/55**LI**	123,572 Derby
	R3345 Atomiser and bogie lubrication
	R3400 Manganese liners to intermediate rubbing plates and buffer faces
6/8/56-5/9/56**GO**	38,117 Derby
	R3698 provision and fitting of new holding down bracket and packing ATC equipment [WR type]
15/10/59-15/2/60**GO**	Swindon BR Green livery

Annual Mileage
1951 7,659
1952 43,112
1953 36,446*
1954 34,089*
1955 25,368*
1956 28,311
1957 35,573
1958 30,700
1959 7,783#
#up to date of transfer to WR 19/4/59
*Includes mileage run whilst on loan to other regions

Boilers
No.857 from new
No.852 5/9/56

Tender
BR1 no.815 from new

Sheds
Chester Midland 27/10/51
Chester West 3/10/53
Cardiff Canton 18/4/59
Shrewsbury 23/4/60
Llanelly 21/5/60
Bristol Barrow Road 14/7/62
Gloucester Barnwood 6/10/62
Gloucester Horton Road 4/5/64
Oxford 11/7/65

Withdrawn 8/65

In truly awful condition, 73021 labours past the shed at Woodford Halse with one of the doomed GC line trains, on 19 April 1965. It carried no shedplate but was officially still at Gloucester Horton Road during this period, hence the WR lamp irons. They have been rearranged in accordance with the overhead line edict but the one on the smokebox door, oddly, is a BR pattern one. On the Western nearly all its life, poor old 73021 went to Oxford after this, where it staggered on for a few weeks before being put out of its misery. Stephen Gradidge.

73022

To traffic 26/10/51

Works
16/10/52-4/11/52**LC**	41,186 Derby Cylinders
9/11/54-7/12/54**LI**	104,037 Derby
	R3400 Manganese liners to intermediate rubbing plates and buffer face
	R3980 Fitting of padded back to fireman's seat
29/5/56-11/6/56**NC[EO]**	43,600 Derby
	ATC equipment [WR type]
8/1/57-8/2/57**GO**	Derby
26/4/58-23/5/58**LC**	Swindon
6/5/59-30/5/59**NC-LC**	70,512 Eastleigh
	Isolating cock, boiler water gauge
	Test W/SW/L157
24/3/60-23/4/60**LI**	85,266 Eastleigh
	5548 Fitting of hinged cab windows
	Modification of briquette tube feeder
	Test W/SW/L157 cancelled
25/4/60-21/5/60**NC**	86,206 Eastleigh
	151 new small tubes 'Stewart and Lloyds' "The Phoenix tubes split during expansion were replaced"
15/8/62-21/9/62**GO**	146,834 Eastleigh
	W/E 15/9/62 awaiting axles
	Water treatment plate fitted to cabside
	T2291 Modification of tender coal hole door plates for improved access
	151 new small tubes 'Stewart and Lloyds'
	Flanges nito arc welded to copper tube plate and copper back plate
4/10/65-4/11/65**LC**	Eastleigh

Annual mileage
1951 6,491
1952 41,531
1953 34,483*
1954 22,637*
1955 33,210*
*Includes mileage run whilst on loan to other regions

Boilers
No.858 from new
No.836 8/2/57
No.1626 22/9/62

Tenders
BR1 no.816
BR1 no.870

Sheds
Chester Midland 27/10/51
Bristol St. Philips Marsh 31/10/53
Llanelly 26/12/53
Bristol St.Phillips Marsh 30/1/54
Swindon 17/7/54
Weymouth 4/10/58
Eastleigh 12/10/64
Guildford 8/6/65
Nine Elms 27/6/66

Withdrawn 4/67

73022, another Western Region Class 5, in for attention at Derby on 10 December 1954 – like other early ones we've seen so far the lamp irons are conventional BR pattern! Home at this time was Swindon shed, across the line from the works but obviously Derby was the designated works. Amongst the Standards the works varied over the years; eventually all the Britannias were dealt with at Crewe for instance but bigger classes were divided up. The shopping proposal originated with the owning Region and was charged against that Region's accounts. R.J. Buckley, Initial Photographics.

73023

To traffic 5/11/51

Works
8/4/54-11/5/54**LI**	67,488 Derby
	R3345 Atomiser and bogie lubrication
	R3400 Manganese liners to intermediate rubbing plates and buffer face
	R3622 Alterations to spring balancing arrangement and fitting stops to prevent reversing gear jamming
	4175 Cab draught shields and padded back to fireman's seat
13/8/56-14/9/56**GO**	72,549 Derby
	R3698 Modifications to tank holding arrangement
	ATC equipment [WR type]
7/10/58-27/10/58**HI**	65,672 Derby
	R5900 Safety links between engine and tender
15/10/59-25/11/59**HI**	Cardiff Canton
23/3/60-13/5/60**GO**	Doncaster BR Green livery

Annual mileage
1951 6,129
1952 30,580
1953 25,081*
1954 32,221*
1955 27,844*
1956 26,788
1957 31,062
1958 32,149
1959 7,617#
#up to date of transfer
to WR 19/4/59
*Includes mileage run whilst
on loan to other regions

Boilers
No.859 from new
No.838 14/9/56
No.1183 13/5/60

Tenders
BR1 no.817 from new
BR1 no.812 1957

Sheds
Patricroft 10/11/51
Chester West 3/10/53
Cardiff Canton 18/4/59
Llanelly 3/5/60
Bath Green Park 22/6/64
Oxford 12/10/64

Withdrawn 8/65

73024

To traffic 15/11/51

Works
11/12/51-28/12/51**NC[EO]**	1,425 Crewe
	Damage, E1871 Discharge of continuous blowdown into ashpan
16/3/53-25/3/53**NC[EO]**	38,755 Crewe
	R3622 Alterations to spring balancing arrangement and fitting stops to stop reversing gear jamming
7/7/53-12/8/53**LC**	44,962 Derby
	4175 Cab draught shields and padded back to fireman's seat
1/5/55-16/6/55**LI**	92,818 Derby
	R3345 Atomiser and bogie lubrication
26/10/55-8/11/55**LC**	10,806 Derby
20/8/56-23/8/56**NC[EO]**	37,446 Derby ATC equipment [WR type]
15/5/57-18/6/57**GO**	65,496 Derby
2/9/59-18/2/60**HI**	Swindon BR Green Livery

Annual mileage
1951 1,720
1952 30,671
1953 26,687*
1954 27,221*
1955 21,644
1956 35,470
1957 37,909
1958 26,909
1959 8,397#
#up to date of transfer
to WR 19/4/59
*Includes mileage run whilst
on loan to other regions

Boilers
No.860 from new
No.849 18/6/57
No.1001 16/12/61

Tender
BR1 no.818 from new

Sheds
Patricroft 17/11/51
Chester West 3/10/53
Shrewsbury 9/10/54
Cardiff Canton 14/7/56
Chester West 13/9/58
Cardiff Canton 18/4/59
Shrewsbury 23/4/60
Bristol Barrow Road 14/7/62
Gloucester Barnwood 6/10/62
Shrewsbury 6/4/63
Llanelly 28/9/63
Bristol Barrow Road 22/6/64
Oxford 12/10/64

Withdrawn 11/64

73024 ready for delivery to its first shed, Patricroft, at Derby on 21 November 1951; nicely burnished chime whistle. R.J. Buckley, Initial Photographics.

73025

To traffic 19/11/51

Works
3/4/52-12/5/52**LC[EO]**	15,474 Derby
18/11/52-19/11/52**NC[EO]**	45,153 Horwich
25/8/53-23/9/53**LC**	77,273 Derby
	R3400 Manese liners to intermediate rubbing plates and buffer faces
	R3622 Alterations to Spring balancing arrangement and fitting stops to prevent reversing gear jamming
	4175 Cab draught shields and padded back to fireman's seat
22/7/55-23/8/55**LI**	142,079 Derby P and V exam
5/12/55-20/12/55**LC**	7,893 Derby
12/6/56-27/6/56**NC[EO]**	23,879 Derby ATC equipment [WR type]
19/11/56-3/1/57**GO**	37,237 Derby
	R5900 Safety links between engine and tender
28/5/58-5/6/58**LC[EO]**	44,279 Caerphilly
5/8/59-16/10/59**HI**	Wolverhampton
2/12/59-10/12/59**NC**	Wolverhampton
	P/E 3/11/62 R6132 Protection shield over leading axle
1/8/63-29/9/63**LC**	Crewe
4/6/65-28/8/65**LI**	Cowlairs

Annual mileage
1951 5,191
1952 44,905
1953 39,712*
1954 39,732*
1955 20,461*
1956 29,314
1957 38,644
1958 16,566
1959 6,734#
#up to date of transfer to WR 19/4/59

Boilers
No.861 from new
No.847 3/1/57

Tender
BR1 no.819 from new

Sheds
Blackpool 24/11/51
Shrewsbury 26/9/53
Cardiff Canton 17/7/54
Chester West 13/9/58
Shrewsbury 18/4/59
Oxley 23/1/65
Shrewsbury 6/3/65
Agecroft 30/4/66
Patricroft 22/10/66

Withdrawn 14/10/67

73025, its sand pipe to the rear of the middle driving wheel clearly needing some adjustment, new at Derby on the same day, 21 November 1951. R.J. Buckley, Initial Photographics.

73026

To traffic 27/11/51

Works
20/11/52-25/11/52**NC[EO]**	41,718 Horwich
19/10/54-10/11/54**LI**	116,302 Derby
	R3345 Atomiser and bogie lubrication
	R3400 Manganese liners to intermediate rubbing plates and buffer faces
	R3622 Alterations to spring balancing arrangement and fitting stops to prevent reversing gear jamming
	R3980 Fitting of padded back to fireman's seat
	5/4175 Cab draught shields and padded back to fireman's seat
25/9/56-2/10/56**NC[EO]**	Derby 4983 ATC equipment
13/2/57-21/3/57**GO**	71,340 Derby
12/2/58-6/5/58**LC**	42,500 Swindon
10/11/59-7/4/60**GO**	Swindon BR Green Livery
28/4/62**GO**	Doncaster [incomplete entry]
9/6/64-9/7/64**LC**	Darlington
21/5/65-21/6/65**LI**	Cowlairs

Annual mileage
1951 4,050
1952 43,855
1953 40,984*
1954 33,736*
1955 32,511*
1956 28,769
1957 42,069
1958 30,726
1959 7,137#
#up to date of transfer to WR 19/4/59

Boilers
No.865 from new
No.857 21/3/57
No.1909 7/4/60
No.1506 24/8/62

Tender
BR1 no.820 from new

Sheds
Blackpool 1/12/51
Shrewsbury 19/9/53
Cardiff Canton 17/7/54
Chester West 13/9/58
Shrewsbury 18/4/59
Leamington Spa 24/10/64
Tyseley 19/6/65
Bolton 30/4/66

Withdrawn 1/4/67

73026 at Cardiff General on 30 August 1956; it had started life as a London Midland loco but had moved to Canton in 1954. Once there, it got WR lamp irons. Stephen Gradidge.

Draught screen flapping in the wind, 73026, still a Shrewsbury locomotive, with a train for Manchester London Road at Stockport on 17 August 1959. Note non-WR lamp irons, while there's something definitely non-standard about the lettering style of that smokebox numberplate... The theory is that the Shrewsbury Class 5s, and particularly the Caprottis, were actually allocated to the former LMS 'half' of the shed and remained firmly in that pool of LM locos, working mainly LM diagrams.

Green 73026 at home at Shrewsbury on 2 September 1962. The shed was rather favoured over the years when it came to new or nearly new BR locomotives; it got a batch of brand new Caprottis for instance as well as 75000 4-6-0s. Photograph Stephen Gradidge.

73027

To traffic 18/12/51

Works
25/11/52-26/11/52**NC[EO]**	50,697 Horwich
3/11/53-26/11/53**LI**	86,996 Derby
	R3345 Atomiser and bogie lubrication
	R3400 Maganes liners to rubbing plates and buffer faces
	R3622 Alterations to spring balancing arrangement and fitting stops to prevent reversing gear jamming
	4175 Cab draught shields and padded back to fireman's seat
	3 brick arch studs
16/11/56-21/12/56**GO**	79,065 Derby
	R5900 Safety links between engine and tender
5/11/57-13/12/57**LC**	Swindon
30/10/59-2/6/60**GO**	Swindon BR Green Livery

Annual mileage
1951 1,255
1952 54,575
1953 33,469*
1954 28,705*
1955 30,252*
*Includes miles run whilst on loan

Boilers
No.863 from new
No.857 21/12/56

Tender
BR1 no.822 from new

Sheds
Blackpool 22/12/51
Bristol St Philips Marsh 3/10/53
Swindon 17/7/54

Withdrawn 2/1964

73028

To traffic 28/12/51

Works
27/11/52-29/11/52**NC[EO]**	46,583 Horwich
23/3/53-8/4/53**LC**	61,582 Derby
16/11/53-31/12/53**LC[EO]**	86,189 Derby
	4175 Cab draught shields and padded back to fireman's seat
1/9/55-26/9/55**LI**	133,225 Derby
	R3622 Alteration to spring balancing arrangement and fitting stops to prevent reversing gear jamming
	R3345 Atomiser and bogie lubrication
	R3400 Manganese liners to intermediate rubbing plates and buffer faces
28/6/56-4/7/56**NC[EO]**	20,779 Derby ATC equipment [WR type]
20/8/57-20/9/57**GO**	Derby
7/10/59-3/10/59**LI-HI**	60,196 Eastleigh
	Blowdown valve operating gear steam brake pipes hinged windows and cab front safety chains between engine and tender isolating cock piston rod packing
	490 monel metal stays riveted over 500 new nuts
	31 new small tubes 'Stewart and Lloyds' 32 rivets repaired in Foundation Ring
29/6/62-11/8/62**GO**	143,000 Eastleigh New firebox back plate 2 fusible plugs
19/11/64-23/12/64**LC**	Eastleigh MR loco
	2 fusible plugs

Annual mileage
1952 50,334
1953 35,855*
1954 28,707*
1955 26,837*
*Includes miles run whilst on loan

Boilers
No.862 from new
No.853 20/9/57
No.854 11/8/62

Tender
BR1 no.822 from new

Sheds
Blackpool 29/12/51
Bristol St. Philips Marsh 3/10/53
Bath Green Park 14/6/58
Bristol Barrow Road 16/7/60
Bath Green Park 8/10/60
Bristol Barrow Road 20/5/61
Swindon 30/11/63
Gloucester Barnwood 25/1/64
Gloucester Horton Road 4/5/64
Oxley 7/11/64
Bolton 30/4/66

Withdrawn 10/12/66

73029

To traffic 17/1/52

Works
13/10/52-20/10/52**NC[EO]**
22/10/52-19/11/52**LC[EO]**
5/6/53-24/6/53**LC**
14/11/55-17/12/55**HI**

35,315 Crewe
35,315 Derby
63,119 Derby
120,446 Derby
R3345 Atomiser and bogie lubrication
R3622 Alterations to spring balancing arrangement and fitting stops to prevent reversing gear jamming

5/11/56-12/11/56**NC[EO]**
24/3/58-2/5/58**GO**
6/10/60-29/10/60**LI-HI**
27/5/63-27/7/63**GO**

27,696 Derby 4983 ATC equipment
68,559 Derby 620 monel metal stays riveted over 620 nuts renewed
76,137 Eastleigh
147,998 Eastleigh
T2238 [cancelled]
W/E 6/7/63 Modifications to horn line
SR type fusible plugs BR Green livery

23/12/64-26/1/65**NC**   Eastleigh
7/8/66-13/9/66**LC**   Eastleigh

Annual mileage
1952 43,275
1953 32,163*
1954 24,937*
1955 20,486*
*Includes miles run whilst on loan

Boilers
No.864 from new
No.994 2/5/58
No.1761 27/7/63

Tender
BR1 no.823 from new

Sheds
Blackpool 19/1/52
Bristol St. Philips Marsh 3/10/53
Carmarthen 26/12/53
Bristol St. Philips Marsh 30/1/54
Swindon 5/10/57
Weymouth 4/10/58
Eastleigh 14/9/64
Guildford 8/5/65
Nine Elms 12/6/66

Withdrawn 7/7/67

Blackpool's 73029 in for attention at Derby on 13 June 1953; a bump may be the reason, from the look of that front end. R.J. Buckley, Initial Photographics.

73030

To traffic 20/6/53

Works
1/1/55-15/1/55**LI**	Derby
	Brake gear
7/11/55-24/11/55**LI**	88,635 Derby
2/1/56-14/1/56**NC[Rect]**	Derby
	Axleboxes
3/2/56-16/2/56**NC[Rect]**	3,842 Derby
	Timken boxes
3/5/57-12/6/57**LC[EO]**	61,182 Derby
	Wheels
	E3329 Modified pistons for continuous blowdown valve
	R5900 Safety links between engine and tender
16/12/57-22/1/58**GO**	94,534 Derby
28/4/59-13/5/59**LC[EO]**	52,196 Derby
	Special exam
25/9/59-26/10/59**HI**	65,288 Derby
	E4983 ATC equipment
30/11/62-17/1/63**GO**	Derby
	R4542 Additional cross bracings to frame

Annual mileage
1953 15,687
1954 40,244
1955 35,334
1956 44,002
1957 47,902
1958 39,936
1959 33,207
1960 38,952

Boilers
No.993 from new
No.865 22/1/58

Tender
BR1 no.864 from new

Sheds
Rugby Testing Plant 11/7/53
Derby 28/11/53
Leicester Midland 13/1/58
Patricroft 20/4/58
Exmouth Jct. 6/10/63
Bristol [Barrow Road] 12/10/64
Bath Green Park 21/2/65
Bristol Barrow Road 7/3/65
Oxford 11/7/65

Withdrawn 8/65

The two air braked Class 5s, 73030 and 73031 ready with their special fitted mineral wagons, at Toton on 24 January 1954.

A brand new 73030 at Derby shed on 19 June 1953. Speedometers were now fitted from new. The middle flexible hose is the air brake connection; air tank slung under the running plate by the firebox. For some reason a shunters pole sits at the front. R.J. Buckley, Initial Photographics.

73031

To traffic 3/7/53

Works
8/10/53	Brakes/steam vacuum or Westinghouse on trial
6/11/53-16/11/53	Derby Brake work
28/2/55-10/3/55**LC**	64,879 Derby
15/2/56-12/3/56**LI**	101,261 Derby
14/2/57-12/3/57**LI**	Derby
29/4/57-16/5/57**LC[EO]**	50,486 Derby
	E3329 Modified pistons for continuous blowdown valves
9/11/57-23/12/57**GO**	81,936 Derby
	R5900 Safety links between engine and tender
	R6132 Fitting of protective shield over tender leading axle
30/12/57-22/1/58**NC[Rect]**	82 Derby Elements
7/60	Swindon BR Green livery

Annual mileage
1953 19,831
1954 40,104
1955 37,664
1956 39,947
1957 45,733

Boilers
No.994 from new
No.862 23/12/57

Tender
BR1 no.865 from new

Sheds
Derby 14/11/53
Bristol Barrow Road 25/5/57
Rugby Testing station 25/1/58
Bath Green Park 2/12/61
Gloucester [Barnwood] 21/4/62
Gloucester [Horton Road] 4/5/64
Oxford 11/7/65

Withdrawn 9/65

Both 73030 and 73031 came out new with the air brake gear and it was taken off after the test runs were deemed to be over. The trials, with the Class 5s and Britannias, did not really lead anywhere, for the problems inherent in equipping even part of the mineral wagon fleet for the Midland coal workings to London were insurmountable. All the wagons had to be tripped in (unfitted) from often outdated collieries only to be broken up again and tripped, unfitted once again, to innumerable yards across London. Just as the pits often had no modern means of loading the wagons, so did the yards in which the wagons end up lack the means to unload them except by hand. Such inbuilt inefficiencies rendered the expense of fitted mineral wagons not worth it. The idea was only really put into practice, to good effect, when Merry Go Round workings were established. Then, the wagons didn't need the constant bothersome breaking of the vacuum – they had air brakes from the first and didn't even stop moving. Driver Bill Webb took the photos, allowing his Fireman to strike this proud pose. Photograph courtesy Rod Fowkes.

73031, still with its Westinghouse pumps, passing Napsbury on 8 August 1953. In between trials, and until the first works visit once they had been concluded, the two Class 5s worked on ordinary duties like this. Stephen Gradidge.

73032

To traffic 10/7/53

Works
30/7/56-24/8/56**LI**	99,639 Derby
	R5900 Safety links between engine and tender
12/11/56-29/11/56**NC[EO]**	5,889 Derby
	E3329 Modified pistons for continuous blowdown valves
31/7/58-14/8/58**LC**	49,410 Derby
7/4/59-15/5/59**GO**	65,105 Derby
13/6/59-30/7/59**LC[EO]**	80,405 Crewe
16/5/60-10/6/60**LC[EO]**	30,158 Derby
16/5/63-6/8/63**HI**	Derby
11/64	Darlington BR Green livery

Annual mileage
1958 12,226
1959 26,879
1960 27,161

Boilers
No.995 from new
No.1007 15/5/59

Tender
BR1 no.866 from new

Sheds
Kingmoor 11/7/53
Bristol St. Philips Marsh 3/10/53
Birkenhead 14/6/58
Willesden 8/5/60
Neasden 9/10/60
Woodford Halse 30/6/62
Nuneaton 18/7/64
Croes Newydd 22/5/65

Withdrawn 7/8/65

73032 new on 17 July 1953. It was destined for Kingmoor, then on the Scottish Region and after that the Western Region. Any reader who in decades past tried to get into Derby shed without permission will be comforted by the fact that the photographer, who was actually a railway employee *in the works* needed a guide every time he took a lunchtime stroll around the adjacent shed to see the new engines he had been working on in steam. On the two or three times he tried it without a guide he was stopped! R.J. Buckley, Initial Photographics.

73033

To traffic 7/8/53

Works
9/11/55-8/12/55**LI**	92,017 Derby MDL/1411
28/6/56-11/7/56**NC[EO]**	Derby
	P/E 15/6/57 E3329 Modified pistons for continuous blowdown valves
7/11/57-29/1/58**LC**	57,547 Wolverhampton
28/5/59-2/7/59**GO**	93,520 Derby
	R5900 Fitting of safety links between engine and tender
2/5/61-8/6/61**HI**	70,479 Derby
30/9/64-19/11/64**HI**	Darlington
	E4983 ATC equipment
12/2/65-16/2/65**LC**	Eastleigh MR loco

Annual mileage
1958 25,39
1959 30,789
1960 37,875

Boilers
No.999 from new
No.1000 2/7/59

Tender
BR1 no.867 from new

Sheds
Polmadie 8/8/53
Shrewsbury 20/9/53
Oxley 3/11/56
Wrexham 14/6/58
Chester Midland 26/9/59
Willesden 14/5/60
Chester Midland 9/6/62
Willesden 16/6/62
Chester Midland 28/7/62
Willesden 11/8/62
Bletchley 7/3/64
Oxley 16/1/65
Nuneaton 6/3/65
Patricroft 24/7/65

Withdrawn 27/1/68

Clean and bright, there was little to equal Riddles' 'BR LNW' livery and here it is to beautiful effect on 73033 at Polmadie in August 1953. Polmadie and the other Scottish sheds do not seem to have fitted the small snow ploughs that Perth adopted. Excellent illustration of the feed pipe from the header, to the whistle and for atomiser steam for the lubricators below, disappearing below the running plate. A pipe leads further to the steam lance cock at the smokebox rim. The operating cable for the whistle can just be seen emerging from the hollow handrail. J. Robertson, www.transporttreasury.co.uk

73034

To traffic 14/8/53

Works
12/8/55-8/9/55**LI**   86,571 Derby
17/10/56-31/10/56**NC[EO]**   Derby
                               P/E 15/6/57 E3329 Modified pistons for continuous blowdown valves
7/1/58-14/2/58**LC**   Wolverhampton
3/11/58-6/2/59**LI**   Swindon BR Green Livery
7/3/60-26/4/60**HC**   Doncaster
1/5/64-24/11/64**HI**   Swindon

Boilers
No.996 from new
No.11845/5/62

Tenders
BR1 no.868 from new
BR1 no.812 7/4/56
BR1 no.817 4/11/57

Sheds
Kingmoor 14/8/53
Shrewsbury 20/9/53
Oxley 3/11/56
Shrewsbury 14/6/58
Agecroft 30/4/66
Patricroft 22/10/66

Withdrawn 16/3/68

73035

To traffic 24/8/53

Works
12/12/55-3/1/56**LI**   93,736 Derby
14/8/56-20/8/56   24,251 Derby
                               4983 ATC equipment
                               P/E 15/6/57 E3329 modified pistons for continuous blowdown valves
11/11/57-17/1/58**LC**   Wolverhampton
7/4/59-12/6/59**HI**   Swindon BR Green livery
4/1/62**GO**   Doncaster [entry incomplete]
13/5/64-8/8/64**LI**   Darlington
16/7/65-11/9/65**HC[EO]**   Cowlairs
                               New boiler

Tender
BR1 no.869 from new

Sheds
Polmadie 24/8/53
Shrewsbury 20/9/53
Oxley 3/11/56
Shrewsbury 14/6/58
Patricroft 18/7/65

Withdrawn 20/1/68

73036

To traffic 1/9/53

Works
13/12/55-9/1/56**LI**	98,100 Derby
23/8/56-29/8/56**NC[EO]**	23,997 Derby
	4983 ATC equipment
	P/E 15/6/57 E3329 Modified pistons for continuous blowdown valve
28/4/58-20/6/58**LC**	Swindon
14/1/59-14/4/59**HI**	Swindon BR Green Livery
4/3/60-7/4/60**LC**	Wolverhampton
1/5/64-22/5/64**LC**	Eastleigh

Boilers
No.1184 from new
No.1617 3/3/62

Tenders
BR1 no.870 from new
BR1 no.816

Sheds
Kingmoor 1/9/53
Shrewsbury 20/9/53
Tyseley 3/11/56
Shrewsbury 25/1/58

Withdrawn 25/9/65

73037

To traffic 8/9/53

Works
2/3/56-28/3/56**LI**	93,985 Derby
	P/E 15/6/57 E3329 Modified pistons for continuous blowdown valves
	MDL/1330
	MDL/1346 Tender axles treated with zinc rich primer and black enamel to reduce corrosion
6/6/58-5/9/58**HC**	Wolverhampton
4/1/60-25/3/60**HI**	Wolverhampton BR Green livery
20/4/61-3/8/61**HC**	Wolverhampton
20/1/64-29/2/64**LI**	Eastleigh WR loco
21/5/65-1/6/65**LC**	Eastleigh
12/9/66-13/9/66**NC**	Eastleigh

Boiler
No.851 3/8/61

Tender
BR1 no.871 from new

Sheds
Shrewsbury 8/9/53
Tysley 3/11/56
Shrewsbury 25/1/58
Llanelly 21/4/62
Bristol Barrow Road 22/6/64
Oxford 12/10/64
Eastleigh 12/4/65
Guildford 8/6/65
Nine Elms 27/6/66

Withdrawn 7/67

Long after the end of steam at London Victoria and very close to the end of Southern steam, 73037 runs in with empty stock for a special, 12 March 1967. Various mortifications were inflicted on steam locos in the last years, only encouraged by the shocking level of official neglect; who was the idiot SPIDER for instance? And as for that front number... 73037 was one of several Class 5s with 1A tenders (regarded when built as carrying insufficient water for the trough-less SR) to work on the Southern, though this one didn't arrive (from Oxford) until 1965. Partly masked by steam is a short reach rod to the mechanical lubricator. Peter Groom.

73038

To traffic 12/9/53

Works
7/9/56-4/10/56**LI**	99,967 Derby
	P/E 15/6/57 E3329 Modified pistons for continuous blowdown valves
15/1/59-17/2/59**GO**	66,949 Derby
	MDL/1380 Firebox mattress made of glass weave
	MDL/1414 Shot peened laminated springs on coupled wheels
25/8/59-31/8/59**NC[EO]**	18,181 Derby
5/9/61-6/10/61**HI**	86,726 Derby
	E4983 ATC equipment
	R5900 Safety links between engine and tender
22/8/63-17/10/63**HC**	Crewe

Annual mileage
1956 35,950
1957 25,754
1958 31,355
1959 29,653
1960 39,462

Boilers
No.1000 from new
No.1005 17/2/59

Tender
BR1 no.872 from new

Sheds
Kingmoor 12/9/53
Chester Midland 9/4/60
Llandudno Jct. 17/11/62
Willesden 2/11/63
Bletchley 13/3/64
Oxley 16/1/65
Nuneaton 6/3/65
Shrewsbury 24/7/65

Withdrawn 2/10/65

A Chester Class 5, 73038, at Cardiff General on 28 August 1956. Stephen Gradidge.

73039

To traffic 25/9/53

Works
17/12/56-24/12/56**NC[EO]**	Derby
	4983 ATC gear
4/1/57-28/11/57**GO**	106,864 Derby
	E3329 modified pistons for continuous blowdown valves
	R5900 safety links between engine and tender
	R6132 Fit protection shields
11/8/58-1/9/58**LC[EO]**	3,381 Derby
21/4/59-6/5/59**LC**	41,716 Derby
7/6/60-4/7/60**LI**	71,407 Derby
7/4/61-2/5/61**HC**	27,283 Derby
	E4983 ATC equipment
4/5/62-1/6/62**LC**	Derby
24/8/64-13/10/64**LI-HI**	Eastleigh MR loco
	W/E 3/10/64 work out of balance wheelshop
	Rivets studs and seams caulked 2 fusible plugs
	Internal boiler exam on frames

Annual mileage
1958 29,058
1959 29,999
1960 29,857

Boilers
No.1001 from new
No.860 28/11/57

Tender
BR1 no.873 from new

Sheds
Bristol St. Philips Marsh 3/10/53
Birkenhead 14/6/58
Willesden 14/5/60
Bletchley 7/3/64
Nuneaton 9/1/65
Patricroft 24/7/65

Withdrawn 9/9/67

73040

To traffic 5/10/53

Works
20/3/56-12/4/56**LI**	107,071 Derby
10/9/58-17/10/58**GO**	10,032 Derby R5900 Safety links between engine and tender
21/10/59-4/11/59**NC/EO**	45,253 Derby E4983 ATC equipment
29/6/60-10/8/60**HI**	70,767 Derby
28/12/62-29/1/63**GO**	Derby
28/8/63-19/9/63**LC**	Crewe
12/65	Eastleigh BR Green livery

Annual mileage
1953 11,057
1954 45,718
1955 40,898
1956 40,066
1957 45,569
1958 42,665
1959 41,965
1960 33,527

Boilers
No.1005 from new
No.993 17/10/58

Tender
BR1 no.874 from new

Sheds
Chester Midland 31/10/53
Willesden 2/11/63
Bletchley 7/3/64
Nuneaton 9/1/65
Croes Newydd 24/7/65
Bolton 30/4/66
Patricroft 13/4/68

Withdrawn 11/5/68

73040 potters about at Bolton Trinity Street, 27 March 1968. Latter-day features include electrification flashes, altered front lamp irons, AWS (battery box under cab). A.G. Forsyth, Initial Photographics.

73041

To traffic 14/10/53

Works
16/3/56-10/4/56**LI**	104,277 Derby
	485 nuts renewed
15/8/57-3/9/57**HI**	58,372 Derby
	300 nuts renewed 12 brick arch studs
16/11/57-19/11/57**NC[EO]**	10,456 Derby
	Timken wheel bearings
26/11/57-4/12/57**NC[EO]**	10,562 Derby
8/10/58-8/11/58**GO**	211,089 Eastleigh
	Blowdown valve operating gear Isolating cock
	T2299 Fitting of smokebox door stop chains
	M/D/L 1377 Bogie bolster slide pads [renewed]
9/4/59-1/5/59**NC**	6,867 Ashford
	4983 ATC equipment
	Modification of briquette tube feeder
	SLB/DN/9/674 Draught screens
9/6/61-1/7/61**LC**	86,064 Eastleigh
	M/D/L 1308 [undisturbed]
8/8/62-8/9/62**LI-HI**	115,840 Eastleigh
	5548 hinged cab windows
	M/D/L 1308 [undisturbed]

Annual mileage
1953 9,854
1954 42,831
1955 44,127
1956 40,987
1957 37,301

Boiler
No.1006 from new
No.1871 8/11/58

Tender
BR1 no.875 from new

Sheds
Chester Midland 31/10/53
Holyhead 22/6/57
Stewarts Lane 14/6/58
Nine Elms 14/6/59
Weymouth 26/11/59
Eastleigh 18/3/61
Weymouth 3/5/61
Eastleigh 14/9/64
Guildford 8/6/65

Withdrawn 6/65

73041 at Eastleigh on 24 March 1963; short lubricator reach rod and no hint of electrification flashes; 73041 was another of the arrivals on the Southern to run with a 1A tender. Stephen Gradidge.

73042

To traffic 22/10/53

Works
11/4/56-3/5/56**LI**	103,473 Derby
12/9/57-17/10/57**HI**	59,353 Derby
	R5900 safety links between engine and tender
	287 nuts renewed 2 brick arch flanges welded
30/9/58-1/11/58**LC**	203,707 Eastleigh
	160 monel metal stays renewed 160 nuts renewed
	2 fusible plugs
19/10/59-14/11/59**GO**	234,539 Eastleigh
	M/D/L 1308 matress fitted
	4983 ATC equipment,
	T2263 Piston rod modified packing
	Isolating cock Hinged windows and windscreen Steam brake pipes,
	Blowdown valve and gear Injector overflow pipes
	M/D/L 1337 and 1346 both cancelled
24/5/62-16/6/62**LI**	70,263 Eastleigh
	Test M/D/L 1308 [undisturbed]

Annual mileage
1953 9,184
1954 44,301
1955 38,954
1956 41,212
1957 37,966

Boilers
No.1002 from new
No.1606 14/11/59

Tender
BR1 no.876 from new

Sheds
Chester Midland 31/10/53
Holyhead 10/8/57
Stewarts Lane 13/10/58
Nine Elms 14/6/59
Weymouth 26/11/59
Eastleigh 18/3/61
Weymouth 3/5/61

Withdrawn 8/65

73043

To traffic 30/10/53

Works
12/1/56-31/1/56**LI**	80,428 Derby 572 nuts renewed
13/9/56-11/10/56**LC**	19,357 Derby
20/5/58-5/7/58**HI**	Doncaster 586 monel metal stays renewed
	151 second hand small tubes
12/7/61-18/8/61**GO**	Doncaster
29/6/64-21/8/64**LI**	Eastleigh
	Manual blowdown gear modified Internal
	Boiler exam on frames

Annual mileage
1953 6,950
1954 37,912
1955 35,143
1956 26,970
1957 36,890

Boilers
No.1008 from new
No.1181 18/8/61

Tender
BR1 no.877 from new

Sheds
Patricroft 30/10/53
Grimesthorpe 20/4/58
Canklow 9/4/61
Eastleigh 2/12/62
Feltham 6/1/64
Eastleigh 14/9/64
Guildford 8/6/65
Nine Elms 27/6/66

Withdrawn 7/67

73044

To traffic 9/11/53

Works
7/3/56-9/4/56**LI**   82,774 Derby
19/11/58-29/12/58**GO** 95,301 Derby
                        MDL/1346 Tender axles treated with zinc rich primer and black enamel to reduce corrosion
                        MDL/1414 Shot peened laminated springs on coupled wheels
22/1/59-9/2/59**NC[EO]** 2,352 Derby
                        E4983 ATC equipment
                        R5900 Safety links between engine and tender
                        R6132 Fitting of protective shield over tender leading axle
24/3/59-7/4/59**LC[TO]** 5,061 Derby
17/11/61-20/12/61**HI** Derby

Annual mileage
1953 6,018
1954 39,051
1955 32,160
1956 31,360
1957 36,280
1958 33,206
1959 36,767
1960 32,010

Sheds
Patricroft 28/11/53
Exmouth Junction 6/10/63
Oxford 10/1/65

Withdrawn 3/65

Boiler
No.1007 from new

Tender
BR1 no.878 from new

73044 in fairly grim condition at Oxford, 15 May 1965. It is, according to the record, already withdrawn but with its smokebox numberplate still up and that full tender you'd have to wonder... Stephen Gradidge.

73045

To traffic 18/11/53

Works
10/1/56-30/1/56**LI**	104,433 Derby
14/5/56-30/5/56**NC[EO]**	12,056 Derby
	Trailing bearings
25/5/57-15/6/57**LC**	164,245 Doncaster
	E3329 Modified pistons for continuous blowdown valve
15/4/58-20/5/58**HI**	201,109 Doncaster
26/11/59-13/1/60**HI**	70,821 Derby
	MDL/1346 Tender axles treated with zinc rich primer and black enamel to reduce corrosion
9/1/61-20/2/61**LC[EO]**	48,661 Derby
14/2/63-23/3/63**GO**	Derby

Annual mileage
1953 7,114
1954 51,294
1955 44,764
1956 47,467
1957 39,080
1958 45,191
1959 36,942
1960 48,538

Boiler
No.1009 from new

Tender
BR1 no.879 from new

Sheds
Leeds Holbeck 18/11/53
Leicester Central 8/9/59
Neasden 13/6/60
Woodford Halse 30/6/62
Shrewsbury 20/6/64
Nuneaton 19/9/64
Croes Newydd 22/5/65
Patricroft 18/7/65

Withdrawn 26/8/67

73046

To traffic 25/11/53

Works
3/4/56-26/4/56**LI**	99,974 Derby
18/12/56-15/1/57**LC[EO]**	34,086 Derby
	P/E 16/6/57 E3329 Modified pistons for continuous blowdown valves
19/8/58-6/10/58**HI**	Doncaster
11/1/61-15/2/61**GO**	Doncaster
6/11/62-7/12/62**HC**	Derby
	54 copper stays renewed 28 copper stays riveted over 4 brick arch studs
25/2/64-6/3/64**NC**	77,141 Eastleigh

Annual mileage
1953 3,565
1954 46,513
1955 40,879
1956 43,103
1957 44,818

Boilers
No.1010 from new
No.1780 15/2/62

Tender
BR1 no.880 from new

Sheds
Leicester Midland 28/11/53
Millhouses 20/4/58
Canklow 29/4/61
Nine Elms 2/12/62

Withdrawn 9/64

73047

[No cards at the National Archive]

To traffic 8/12/53

Works
13/3/56-7/4/56**LI**	94,291 Eastleigh
	Safety clips to brake hanger pins Overhaul of blowdown valve Cylinder release valves
14/5/57-20/5/57**NC**	144,374 Brighton
25/3/58-3/5/58**LI-HI**	171,724 Eastleigh
	W/E 26/4/58 awaiting new axle
	R5900 Safety chains between engine and tender Blowdown valve operating gear
	T2299 Smokebox chains
	Isolating cock and gear
	T2263 [R] and T2278 [O]
	340 monel metal stays riveted over 340 nuts renewed
	151 new small tubes 'Stewart and Lloyds'
17/3/60-28/5/60**GO**	243,303 Eastleigh
	Injector overflow pipes
	Cab windows and screens
	T2263 [R] T2278 [O] and T2272 [renewed 3 rings both sides]
	486 monel metal stays riveted over 486 nuts renewed
	51 new small tubes 'Stewart and Lloyds'
	2 fusible plugs
28/5/62-16/6/62**LI**	66,611 Eastleigh

Annual mileage
1953 2,252
1954 49,586

Boilers
No.997 from new
No.1623 28/5/60

Tender
BR1 no.881 from new

Sheds
Millhouses 2/1/54
Bath Green Park 12/8/55
Shrewsbury 18/7/64

Withdrawn 5/12/64

73047 approaching the troughs at Melton Mowbray with an up mid-morning train for St Pancras, December 1955. Peter Groom.

73048

To traffic 17/12/53

Works
27/8/56-25/9/56**HI**	113,086 Derby
	P/E 16/6/57 E3329 Modified pistons for continuous blowdown valves
	MDL/1337 Intermediate rubbing plates and plungers with hard surfacing
	of OK Hardtop 8 Electrode on working surfaces
12/9/57-10/10/57**LC**	46,813 Derby
14/8/58-3/10/58**HI**	Doncaster
7/9/60-7/10/60**HI**	160,965 Derby
14/9/63-7/1/63**GO**	Darlington

Annual mileage
1953 1,011
1954 52,569
1955 35,200
1956 37,273
1957 44,656
1958 39,148
1959 40,794
1960 30,990

Boiler
No.1011 from new

Tender
BR1 no.882 from new

Sheds
Millhouses 2/1/54
Chester Midland 6/2/60
Willesden 2/11/63
Bletchley 7/3/64
Nuneaton 9/1/65
Banbury 19/6/65
Bolton 30/4/66

Withdrawn 14/10/67

73049

To traffic 30/12/53

Works
7/11/55-29/11/55**LC**	75,166 Brighton
17/1/57-16/2/57**LI**	119,064 Eastleigh
	220 monel metal stays riveted over 220 nuts renewed
	151 new small tubes 'Stewart and Lloyds'
4/7/57-11/7/57**NC**	134,050 Brighton
25/11/58-20/12/58**GO**	183,620 Eastleigh Blowdown operating gear modified Isolating
	cock fitted Safety chains between engine and tender Smokebox chains
	Reversing shaft modified, Piston rod packing modified
	T2081 Regulator valve seating [new]
	T2263 [reconditioned] T2278 [O]
	T2272 [Heads renewed]
15/10/59-3/12/59**NC**	Bath Green Park
19/4/61-13/5/61**LI-HI**	80,758 Eastleigh
	Hinged cab windows
	T2081 cancelled Additional cross bracing on tender
	420 monel metal stays riveted over 420 nuts renewed
	33 new small tubes 'Stewart and Lloyds'
23/7/63-31/8/63**LI-HI**	152,581 Eastleigh
	485 nuts renewed 151 new small tubes
	WR loco. BR Green livery

Annual mileage
1953 30
1954 43,170

Boilers
No.1012 from new
No.1006 20/12/58

Tender
BR1 no.883 from new

Sheds
Leicester Midland 2/1/54
Bath Green Park 12/8/55
Shrewsbury 4/4/60
Bristol [Barrow Road] 16/6/62
Bath Green Park 14/7/62
Oxford 12/10/64

Withdrawn 3/65

73050

To traffic 14/4/54

Works
14/3/55-26/3/55**LC**	34,818 Eastleigh
3/4/56-27/4/56**LI**	78,041 Eastleigh
7/6/56-19/6/56**LC**	Derby
4/3/57-13/3/57**LC**	116,652 Eastleigh
21/10/57-1/11/57**NC**	135,678 Brighton
10/4/58-10/5/58**LI-HI**	146,702 Eastleigh
	Isolating cock pipes and gear,
	9080 Briquette container modified
	5900 Safety chains between engine and tender
	T2272 Piston heads renewed
20/1/60-27/2/60**GO**	201,733 Eastleigh
	T2081 Regulator valve, stainless steel [O]
	T2263 Piston rod packing
	T2272 Piston heads 3 rings [R]
	T2278 Modified steam brake pipes[O]
	5548 Hinged cab windows
	Overflow pipes
	380 monel metal stays riveted over 380 nuts renewed
	15 new large tubes
21/2/62-17/3/63**LC**	69,544 Eastleigh
	T2081 [U] WR loco.
12/6/62-30/6/62**LC**	71,165 Eastleigh
	T2081 [O]
15/6/64-12/8/64**LI**	Eastleigh MR loco
	W/E 18/8/64 heavy boiler work
	470 monel metal stays riveted over 470 nuts renewed
	151 new small tubes 'Stewart and Lloyds'

Boiler
No.1619 27/12/60

Tender
BR1G no.989 from new

Sheds
Bath Green Park 13/5/54
Gloucester [Barnwood] 11/8/62
Bath Green Park 17/11/62
Llanelly 13/4/64
Shrewsbury 25/4/64
Agecroft 30/4/66
Patricroft 22/10/66

Withdrawn 7/68 Engine preserved

73050 running light at Wellow, on the Somerset and Dorset, 14 May 1960. 73050, 73051 and 73052 were unusual in going as a batch (BR and its predecessors preferred to do things in fives) of three. They went to the Southern Region which then had charge of Bath Green Park. The shed passed to the Western Region and the Class 5s along with it in 1958 and though 73050 moved away (it is now preserved) the other two stayed at Bath until withdrawn. From this loco onwards coupling rods were plain section. Stephen Gradidge.

Before it got to Bath Green Park 73050 was an exhibit for the International Railway Congress; here it is amid fellow Standards in the Willesden roundhouse on 28 May 1954.

73051

To traffic 10/5/54

Works
15/3/55-26/3/55**LC**	39,100 Eastleigh
17/2/56-18/2/56**NC-LC**	68,543 Eastleigh
16/4/56-2/5/56**NC**	Derby
2/5/57-25/5/57**LI**	110,904 Eastleigh
10/4/59-9/5/59**GO**	180,571 Eastleigh
	5900 Safety chains between engine and tender
	Isolating cock Smokebox chains, Blowdown gear modified
	T2263 Piston rod packing [R]
	T2272 Piston heads, new 3 rings
	T2278 Modified steam brake pipes [O]
15/9/61-14/10/61**LI-HI**	85,063 Eastleigh
	5548 Cab windows modified
16/1/63-26/1/63**LC**	126,036 Eastleigh
	WR loco.
13/8/63-21/9/63**LI**	144,756 Eastleigh BR Green livery
	WR loco.

Boilers
No.1168 from new
No.1906 9/5/59

Tender
BR1G no.990 from new

Shed
Bath Green Park 22/6/54

Withdrawn 8/65

73051, in typically dire external condition, at Oxford on 15 May 1965, a few months before withdrawal. Stephen Gradidge.

73052

To traffic 20/5/54

Works
28/2/55-5/3/55**LC**	38,373 Eastleigh
21/2/56-10/3/56**LI**	77,380 Eastleigh
1/5/56-21/5/56**LC**	Derby
	Balancing
25/11/57-6/12/57**NC**	148,381 Brighton
16/5/58-14/6/58**LI-HI**	160,070 Eastleigh
	5900 Safety chains between engine and tender
	Isolating cock and equipment Blowdown valve operating equipment Piston rod packing
	T2272 Piston heads renewed 3 rings both sides
23/6/58-6/8/58**LC**	Nine Elms
10/11/59-30/11/59**NC**	Bath Green Park
21/1/60-9/2/60**NC**	Bath Green Park
31/5/60-25/6/60**GO**	220,509 Eastleigh
	Injector overflow pipes Cab windows and screens
	T2263 Piston rod packing[R]
	T2272 Piston heads [R]
	T2278 Modified steam brake pipes[O]
	T2303 Grease lubricators [O]
19/5/61-12/6/61**NC-LC**	33,059 Eastleigh
19/6/62-28/7/62**LI**	68,634 Eastleigh
	386 monel metal stays riveted over 386 nuts renewed
	2 fusible plugs
7/5/64-3/6/64**LC**	Eastleigh
	WR loco.

Boilers
No.965 from new
No.1621 25/6/60

Tender
BR1G no.991 from new

Shed
Bath Green Park 22/6/54

Withdrawn 12/64

73053

To traffic 4/6/54

Works
1/12/54-8/12/54**LC**	24,127 Derby
28/12/54-7/1/55**NC**	25,614 Derby
14/3/55-14/4/55**LC[EO]**	32,548 Derby
11/2/57-20/3/57**HI**	122,306 Doncaster
5/6/59-17/7/59**GO**	225,733 Doncaster
24/4/61-24/5/61**HI**	70,806 Derby
1/5/62-25/5/62**LC**	Derby
17/10/62-11/2/62**NC**	Derby
21/11/63-29/5/64	Swindon
3/5/65-12/5/65**LC**	Cowlairs

Annual mileage
1954 25,453
1955 46,544
1956 46,921
1957 45,760
1958 40,795
1959 51,656
1960 31,091

Boilers
No.1169 from new
No.1185 17/7/59

Tender
BR1H no.992 from new

Sheds
Leeds Holbeck 4/6/54
Leicester Central 12/9/59
Neasden 18/6/60
Woodfrord Halse 30/6/62
Cricklewood 18/5/63
Bedford 6/7/63
Woodford Halse 3/8/63
Shrewsbury 18/7/64
Patricroft 24/7/65

Withdrawn 9/3/68

73053, carrying what must be the worst, crudest numberplate ever displayed, leaves Wakefield Kirkgate with the 1.50pm Scarborough-Manchester, 12 August 1967. At last we have a good view of the AWS receiver guard plate under the buffer beam. J.L. Stevenson, courtesy Hamish Stevenson.

73054

[No cards at the National Archive]

To traffic 9/6/54

Works
2/11/55-29/11/55**LC**   70,502 Crewe
30/3/57-25/4/57**LI**   132,251 Derby
                     E3329 Modified pistons for continuous blowdown valves
                     R5900 Safety links between engine and tender
9/59   Swindon BR Green Livery
20/9/63-2/11/63**GO**   Eastleigh WR loco. Blowdown gear modified 2 fusible plugs

Annual mileage
1954 31,406
1955 43,801
1956 47,555
1957 56,910

Boilers
No.1170 from new
No.1001 1/8/58
No.1795 8/12/61
No.836 2/11/63

Tender
BR1H no.993

Sheds
Leeds Holbeck 19/6/54
Derby 13/8/55
Bristol Barrow Road 18/5/57
Bath Green Park 22/4/61

Withdrawn 8/65

73054, Holbeck's latest acquisition, brand new at York in 1954. R. Butterfield, Initial Photographics.

73055

To traffic 23/6/54

Works
24/11/55**NC**	St.Rollox
7/1/57-2/2/57**LI**	St.Rollox
27/3/58-2/5/58**LC**	Cowlairs
17/11/58-6/12/58**GO**	Cowlairs
9/1/61-4/3/61**HI**	Cowlairs
29/5/63-6/7/63**GO**	Cowlairs
21/9/65-6/10/65**LC[EO]**	Cowlairs

Tender
BR1H no.994 from new

Shed
Polmadie 7/8/54

Withdrawn 25/5/66

73056

To traffic 2/7/54

Works
5/5/55-12/5/55**LC[EO]**	St.Rollox
29/11/55-30/11/55**NC**	St.Rollox
9/1/56-20/1/56**NC[EO]**	St.Rollox
4/4/56-25/4/56**NC[EO]**	Derby
8/4/57-2/5/57**LI**	St.Rollox
1/6/59-20/6/59**GO**	St.Rollox
12/5/60-13/6/60**NC[EO]**	Cowlairs
17/11/60-24/12/60**LC**	Cowlairs
9/10/61-24/1161**HI**	Cowlairs
11/10/62-2/11/62**LC**	Cowlairs
14/5/63-1/6/63**LC**	Cowlairs

Tender
BR1H no.995 from new

Sheds
Polmadie 2/7/54
Aberdeen Ferryhill 31/7/64

Withdrawn 26/6/65

New 73056, second of a batch of ten for Polmadie, at Derby on 2 July 1954. The red flag means do not move – fitters are about! The arrival of a number of new Standards there; Clans, Britannias, Class 5s and 2-6-4Ts, prompted *The Railway Observer* to contrast the sleek modernity of the Polmadie passenger power with the decrepitude of the occupants on the freight side. R.J. Buckley, Initial Photographics.

73057

To traffic 8/7/54

Works
26/10/54-28/10/54**NC[EO]**	St.Rollox
15/12/54-22/12/54**NC[EO]**	St.Rollox
26/10/55-28/10/55**NC**	St.Rollox
28/4/56-7/6/56**LC[EO]**	Derby
9/2/57-2/3/57**LI**	St.Rollox
17/4/59-15/5/59**GO**	Cowlairs
8/6/59-13/6/59**NC[EO]**	St.Rollox
23/8/61-21/10/61**HI**	Cowlairs
3/8/64-10/10/64**LI**	Cowlairs
3/12/64-19/12/64**NC[EO]**	Cowlairs

Sheds
Polmadie 7/8/54
Corkerhill 22/6/64

Withdrawn 29/3/66

Tenders
BR1H no.996 from new
BR1H no.1002 13/4/61
BR1H no.1001 31/8/61

73057 with a Glasgow-Ayr relief, passing Irvine on 15 July 1957. This would be one of the Scottish Region's blue ground numberplates. J.L. Stevenson, courtesy Hamish Stevenson.

73057 at Derby on 9 July 1954, another Polmadie-bound Class 5. R.J. Buckley, Initial Photographics.

73058

To traffic 13/7/54

Works
15/12/54-18/12/54**NC[EO]**	St.Rollox
18/8/55-9/9/55**LC**	Crewe
6/10/55-21/10/55**LC**	Derby
11/1/56-12/1/56**NC**	St.Rollox
25/6/56-10/7/56**LI**	St.Rollox
23/12/57-28/12/57**LC[TO]**	St.Rollox
28/10/58-27/11/58**GO**	Cowlairs
4/2/60-9/2/60**LC[TO]**	Cowlairs
4/4/60-23/4/60**HC**	Cowlairs
25/5/60-28/5/60**NC[EO]**	Cowlairs
20/10/61-28/10/61**LC[TO]**	Cowlairs
12/9/62-13/10/62**HI**	Cowlairs

Tender
BR1H no.997 from new

Sheds
Polmadie 12/7/54
Aberdeen Ferryhill 31/7/64

Withdrawn 7/11/64

73059

To traffic 13/8/54

Works
20/10/55-22/10/55**NC**	St.Rollox
16/3/57-10/4/57**LI**	St.Rollox
23/9/58-11/10/58**LC[EO]**	Cowlairs
16/2/59-14/3/59**GO**	Cowlairs
18/3/60-15/4/60**HC**	St.Rollox
26/2/62-6/4/62**LI**	Cowlairs
16/9/63-19/10/63**HC[EO]**	Cowlairs
7/9/64-3/10/64**LC**	Cowlairs
11/6/65-3/7/65**LI**	Cowlairs

Boiler
No.1171

Tenders
BR1H no.998 from new
BR1H no.1303
BR1C no.1011

Shed
Polmadie 4/9/54

Withdrawn 1/5/67

73058, in an almost perfect portrait, at Polmadie on 19 March 1955. J. Robertson, www.transporttreasury.co.uk

73059, destined for Polmadie, standing at Derby on 15 August 1954 and a thing of beauty. It was one of a couple in the Polmadie batch that stayed at the big Glasgow shed to the end. R.J. Buckley, Initial Photographics.

73060

To traffic 26/8/54

Works
4/11/55-5/11/55**NC**	St.Rollox
15/4/57-17/5/57**LI**	St.Rollox
10/2/58-1/3/58**LC[EO]**	Cowlairs
8/6/59-27/6/59**GO**	Cowlairs
24/4/61-3/6/61**HI**	Cowlairs
21/8/63-21/9/63**GO**	Cowlairs
11/3/65-17/4/65**NC**	Cowlairs
3/6/65-15/6/65**NC**	Cowlairs

Tender
BR1H no.999 from new

Sheds
Polmadie 4/9/54
Motherwell 25/10/55
Polmadie 26/8/57

Withdrawn 1/5/67

73061

To traffic 2/9/54

Works
10/11/55-11/11/55**NC**	St.Rollox
28/6/56**NC**	St.Rollox
31/7/57-15/8/57**LI**	St.Rollox
10/8/59-5/9/59**GO**	Cowlairs
11/9/59-22/9/59**LC[EO]**	Cowlairs
12/2/62-10/3/62**HI**	Cowlairs
9/7/63-10/7/63**LC[EO]**	Cowlairs
6/8/63**NC[EO]**	Cowlairs
5/6/64**NC[EO]**	Cowlairs

Tenders
BR1H no.1000 from new
BR1H no.1001 31/7/59
BR1H no.1002 30/8/61

Sheds
Polmadie 2/9/54
Motherwell 25/10/55
Polmadie 28/6/57

Withdrawn 23/12/64

73061 new at Derby and Polmadie-bound, 3 September 1954. None of this batch of ten, 73055-73064, was ever based anywhere but in the Scottish Region; in fact only one of the Class 5s – 73006 – sent new to Scotland was ever transferred away from the Region, apart from 73030-73039 allocated to Scotland and diverted soon after or even before arrival. They also moved about within the ScR much less than the English engines moved around south of the border. R.J. Buckley, Initial Photographics.

73062

To traffic 15/9/54

Works
8/11/55-9/11/55**NC**	St.Rollox
27/6/56**NC[EO]**	St.Rollox
15/8/57-31/8/57**LI**	St.Rollox
25/8/59-12/9/59**GO**	Cowlairs
28/2/62-24/3/62**HI**	Cowlairs
4/5/62-14/8/62	Cowlairs
14/8/62-18/8/62**LC[EO]**	Cowlairs
6/8/63**NC[EO]**	Cowlairs
5/3/64-7/3/64**LC[EO]**	Cowlairs

Tenders
BR1H no.1001 from new
BR1H no.1000 31/7/59

Sheds
Polmadie 15/9/54
Motherwell 25/10/55
Polmadie 28/6/57

Withdrawn 26/6/65

73063

To traffic 29/9/54

Works
7/12/55**NC**	St.Rollox
25/6/57-7/8/57**LI**	St.Rollox
4/12/59-27/12/59**LC**	St.Rollox
26/10/59-28/11/59**GO**	Cowlairs
9/12/59-18/12/59**NC[EO]**	Cowlairs
1/9/62-12/10/62**HI**	Cowlairs

Tenders
BR1H no.1002 from new
BR1H no.996 13/2/61

Shed
Polmadie 2/10/54

Withdrawn 23/6/66

73062 at Polmadie shed about 1955, before its transfer to Motherwell; behind is an even newer 2-6-4T. It is well known that the Standards were not well received on the Western Region while the Britannias by contrast were welcomed with open arms on the Great Eastern Section. Arguably it was the Scottish Region that took on board a greater proportion of Standards than other Regions; it tended to concentrate them at certain sheds too. The point really was that they had plenty of obsolete older pre-Group designs against which the stronger new engines could shine. 'Mac' (thought to be Norman McKillop) in 'Scottish Region Magazine' in 1951 penned an article under the heading 'The Standard 5 is Good': *The line of visibility is exceptionally good from both sides of the cab, and everything to make for comfort is there, the only things missing in up-to-the-minute design being electric lighting and the automatic train control apparatus, which is due not to lack of thought on the designer's part but (as everyone knows) to lack of capital.* J. Robertson, www.transporttreasury.co.uk

73064

To traffic 1/10/54

Works
27/12/55-28/12/55**NC**	St.Rollox
29/4/57-1/6/57**HI**	St.Rollox
10/6/59-4/7/59**GO**	Cowlairs
8/9/60-29/10/60**HC[EO]**	Cowlairs
10/5/62-23/6/62**HI**	Cowlairs
5/6/63-12/6/63**NC[EO]**	Cowlairs
13/11/64-14/11/64**NC**	Cowlairs
16/11/64-20/11/64**NC**	Cowlairs
1/6/65-26/6/65**LC[EO]**	Cowlairs
17/2/66-19/3/66**U[EO]**	Cowlairs

Tender
BR1H no.1003 from new

Shed
Polmadie 2/10/54

Withdrawn 1/5/67

Top right. 73064 on an Ayr-Glasgow train near Dalry, 25 July 1959. The type and height of the vacuum pipe on the front beam varied – as between 73064 and 73066 opposite, for instance. J.L. Stevenson, courtesy Hamish Stevenson.

Bottom right. 73066 in its first days as a Holbeck engine about 1955; the old Midland shed at Holbeck passed to the North Eastern Region in October 1956 which meant the abolition of the LM 20A District and the establishment of the NER 55 District.

73065

To traffic 13/10/54

Works
5/11/56-23/11/56**LI**	87,442 Derby
	R5900 Safety links between engine and tender
	E3329 Modified pistons for continuous blowdown valve
	646 nuts renewed 12 brick arch studs 28 new large tubes
29/10/57-7/11/57**LC**	48,438 Derby Tender tank
30/10/58-13/12/58**GO**	Doncaster EDNL/86 Firebox support brackets clearance modified
7/12/59-11/12/59**NC**	Doncaster
23/3/61-6/5/61**GO**	Doncaster
30/10/64-16/12/64**LI**	Eastleigh
	430 monel metal stays riveted over 430 nuts renewed
	Foundation Ring rivets and seams recaulked. 2 fusible plugs

Annual mileage
1954 11,307
1955 42,527
1956 37,955
1957 52,066

Boilers
No.1181 from new
No.1613 6/5/61

Tender
BR1C no.1004 from new

Sheds
Millhouses 16/10/54
Canklow 31/12/61
Eastleigh 17/12/62
Feltham 6/1/64
Nine Elms 20/11/64
Guildford 8/6/65
Nine Elms 27/6/66

Withdrawn 7/7/67

73066

To traffic 15/10/64

Works
4/2/57-13/3/57**HI**	Doncaster
4/1/58-25/1/58**LC**	Doncaster
13/1/59-19/2/59**GO**	195,546 Doncaster
19/5/59-29/5/59**NC[EO]**	Doncaster
19/8/59-17/9/59**LC[EO]**	Doncaster
10/11/59-23/11/59**LC[EO]**	31,848 Derby
29/8/60-27/9/60**LC[EO]**	61,615 Derby
3/10/60-7/10/60**NC[rect EO]**	Derby
12/1/61-21/2/61**LC**	71,486 Derby
24/4/61-17/5/61**LC[EO]**	77,210 Derby
25/6/62-7/8/62**HI**	Derby
8/4/64-17/6/64	Swindon

Annual mileage
1954 10,521
1955 52,547
1956 43,712
1957 45,729
1958 42,870
1959 40,341
1960 31,402

Boilers
No.1182 from new
No.861 19/2/59

Tender
BR1C no.1005 from new

Sheds
Holbeck 16/10/54
Leicester [Central] 6/9/59
Neasden 13/6/60
Leicester [Central] 30/6/62
Woodford Halse 12/1/63
Cricklewood 12/5/63
Leamington 5/10/64
Tyseley 19/6/65
Bolton 30/4/66

Withdrawn 15/4/67

73066 at Bolton shed on 27 July 1966. It moved around as much as any Class 5 and via the Western Region ended its days back on the LMR, at Bolton, where it acquired one of those crude replacement smokebox numbers. C. Stacey, Initial Photographics.

73066 at Cricklewood, its home by then, on 25 July 1964. Peter Groom.

73067

To traffic 22/10/54

Works
9/7/57-21/8/57**LI**	119,160 Derby
	R5900 Safety links between engine and tender
	E3329 Modified pistons for continuous blowdown valves
24/6/59-1/8/59**GO**	83,546 Doncaster
19/6/61-13/7/61**HI**	75,025 Derby
	E4983 ATC equipment
16/10/64-1/12/64**LI-HI**	Eastleigh
	MR loco. W/E 21/11/64 awaiting material, now recieved, work proceeding

Annual mileage
1954 12,198
1955 46,393
1956 40,476
1957 36,898
1958 35,594
1959 32,171
Mileage at 2/1/60 = 208,981
1960 37,963

Boilers
No.1183 from new
No.1169 1/8/59
No.1795 1/12/64

Tender
BR1C no.1006 from new

Sheds
Nottingham 6/11/54
Leicester Midland 22/2/58
Millhouses 10/5/58
Holyhead 6/2/60
Chester Midland 9/2/63
Willesden 2/11/63
Bletchley 7/3/64
Oxley 16/1/65
Shrewsbury 3/4/65
Agecroft 30/4/66
Patricroft 22/10/66

Withdrawn 30/3/68

73068

To traffic 29/10/54

Works
10/9/56-11/10/56**LI**	85,880 Derby
	E3329 Modified pistons for continuous blowdown valves
10-12/58	Swindon BR Green Livery
	EDNL/86 firebox support brackets clearance modified

Annual mileage
1954 9,082
1955 44,915
1956 42,275
1957 56,912

Boilers
No.1184 from new
No.998 7/5/60

Tender
BR1C no.1007 from new

Sheds
Derby 6/11/54
Bristol Barrow Road 5/57
Gloucester [Barnwood] 6/10/62
Bath Green Park 4/5/64
Gloucester [Horton Road] 10/1/65
Bath Green Park 11/4/65

Withdrawn 1/66

73068 at Brighton shed on 5 June 1960, an odd place for a Bristol Barrow Road loco any day of the week; the 'M' indicates a return to the LMR. There must have been some excursions arriving that day, for behind 73068 is one of Bescot's Black Fives, 44910. The BR Class 5 is in green livery, with conventional lamp irons and the WR red spot route indication below the number on the cab. Stephen Gradidge

73069

To traffic 5/11/54

Works
18/12/54-31/12/54**NC**	5,736 Derby Dragbox
13/1/55-9/2/55**LC[EO]**	7,177 Derby
21/1/57-2/3/57**HI**	Doncaster
3/4/59-7/5/59**GO**	198,624 Doncaster
6/10/60-3/11/60**HC**	65,085 Derby
10/11/60-16/11/60**NC[Rect EO]**	Derby Weighing
10/1/63-8/2/63**HI**	Derby
1/8/66-30/9/66**HC**	Crewe Plain Black

Annual mileage
1954 5,775
1955 52,838
1956 47,902
1957 40,255
1958 43,548
1959 47,021
1960 35,613

Boilers
No.1185 from new
No.1189 7/5/59

Tender
BR1C no.1008 from new

Sheds
Derby 6/11/54
Leeds [Holbeck] 4/8/55
Leicester [Central] 6/9/59
Neasden 13/6/60
Leicester [Central] 30/6/62
Woodford Halse 11/2/63
Cricklewood 12/5/63
Leamington 5/10/64
Tyseley 16/6/65
Bolton 30/4/66
Patricroft 13/4/68
Carnforth 1/7/68

Withdrawn 10/8/68

73069 late in the day, in a typical scruffy shed yard of the time. The loco has plain black livery and was the only one in the class thus treated – it was ex-works in December 1966. As such, it was probably the last repaint for them for all time in BR service. Paul Chancellor Collection.

73070

To traffic 12/11/54

Works
27/2/56-1/3/56**NC**	59,937 Derby
12/3/57-1/4/57**LI**	105,875 Derby
	E3329 Modified pistons for continuous blowdown valves
	R5900 Safety links between engine and tender
11/5/57-17/5/57**LC**	3,048 Derby
10/6/57-13/6/57**NC[Rect]**	Derby
13/11/58-2/12/58**LC**	69,271 Derby
20/1/60-26/2/60**GO**	116,824 Derby
	R5548 Hinged cab windows
	E4983 ATC equipment
21/6/62-13/7/62**HI**	Derby
22/10/63-5/11/63**NC**	Horwich

Annual mileage
1954 5,555
1955 48,446
1956 43,837
1957 40,240
1958 39,234
1959 45,204
1960 34,657

Boilers
No.1186 from new
No.1995 26/2/60

Tender
BR1C no.1009 from new

Sheds
Chester Midland 4/12/54
Willesden 2/11/63
Bletchley 7/3/64
Shrewsbury 20/6/64
Bolton 30/4/66

Withdrawn 29/4/67

73070 at Stockport Edgeley. D. Forsyth, Paul Chancellor Collection.

73071

To traffic 19/11/54

Works
22/3/56-17/4/56**NC**	56,075 Doncaster
3/6/57-20/6/57**LI**	90,045 Derby
1/7/57-5/7/57**NC[Rect]**	Derby
	R5900 Safety links between engine and tender
	E3329 Modified pistons for continuous blowdown valves
20/9/57-26/9/57**LC**	10,459 Derby
21/10/57-31/10/57**LC[TO]**	12,719 Derby
15/6/59-7/7/59**LI**	85,894 Derby
	Tender tank
31/10/59-28/11/59**LC**	10,524 Crewe
28/1/60-10/2/60**LC[EO]**	14,942 Derby
	E4983 ATC equipment
22/8/61-6/10/61**GO**	72,652 Derby
	R5548 Hinged cab windows
5/2/64-20/5/64**HI**	Darlington

Annual mileage
1954 5,020
1955 45,928
1956 24,935
1957 34,033
1958 46,217
1959 33,044
1960 34,656

Boilers
No.1187 from new
No.1751 6/10/61

Tender
BR1C no.1010 from new

Sheds
Chester Midland 26/4/57
Kings Cross 18/2/56
Chester Midland 18/5/57
Cricklewood 19/5/63
Bedford 24/6/63
Woodford Halse 3/8/63
Oxley 16/1/65
Shrewsbury 3/4/65
Patricroft 18/7/65

Withdrawn 16/9/67

73072

To traffic 8/12/54

Works
2/1/57-21/1/57**LI**	87.046 Derby
	R5900 Safety links between engine and tender
10/7/57-15/7/57**LC[TO]**	17,516 Derby
21/4/58-7/5/58**NC**	50,795 Derby
29/4/59-22/5/59**GO**	Cowlairs
14/2/62-24/3/62**HI**	Cowlairs
29/1/65-30/1/65**NC[EO]**	Cowlairs
18/3/65-22/5/65**HI**	Cowlairs
2/2/66-5/3/66**LC[EO]**	Cowlairs
26/4/66-7/5/66**NC[EO]**	Cowlairs

Annual mileage
1954 1,895
1955 44,067
1956 41,006
1957 39,612
1958 40,056
1959 10,205 [up to date of transfer to Sc. Reg. 22/3/59]

Boiler
No.1188 from new

Tenders
BR1C no.1011 from new
BR1B no.1303

Sheds
Chester Midland 1/1/55
Polmadie 22/11/58

Withdrawn 27/10/66

Polmadie's 73072 nearly ready in the shed yard at Kingmoor; the driver's oil can is sitting on the running plate at the front. 'Big' Scottish cabside numbers. The pipe feeding steam to the lubricator atomiser has been pulled out and looks quite different from the normal arrangement. W. Hermiston, www.transporttreasury.co.uk

73073

To traffic 16/12/54

Works
6/12/56-27/12/56**LI**	84,647 Derby
	R5900 Safety links between engine and tender
18/2/59-3/4/59**GO**	Doncaster
3/10/61-16/11/61**HI**	96,025 Derby E4983 ATC equipment
28/9/64-6/11/64**LI-HI**	Eastleigh
	Studs and seams caulked 2 brick arch studs 2 fusible plugs

Annual mileage
1954 1,456
1955 45,007
1956 38,184
1957 45,150
1958 38,007
1959 47,294
1960 32,200

Boilers
No.1189 from new
No.1182 3/4/59

Tender
BR1C no.1012 from new

Sheds
Patricroft 1/1/55
Bath [Green Park] 20/4/55
Leicester [Midland] 9/8/55
Millhouses 20/4/58
Holyhead 31/1/60
Llandudno Jct. 7/3/63
Woodford Halse 2/11/63
Nuneaton 18/7/64
Patricroft 18/7/65

Withdrawn 4/11/67

Another one out of the works, 73073 at Derby in December 1954. Derby kept it for the Christmas, sending it on to Patricroft (officially) for 1 January 1955. R.J. Buckley, Initial Photographics.

73074

To traffic 22/12/54

Works
22/12/54	MDL/1329 Modified drainage cocks
3/12/57-23/12/57**LI**	121,759 Derby
	R5900 Safety links between engine and tender
	R6132 Protective shield over tender leading axle
31/7/58-9/8/58**NC**	Doncaster
23/4/59-16/5/59**LC**	Doncaster
14/12/60-17/1/61**GO**	Doncaster

Annual mileage
1954 216
1955 43,904
1956 39,852
1957 38,174

Boilers
No.1190 from new
No.839 17/1/61
N0.846 29/7/64

Tender
BR1C no.1013 from new

Sheds
Patricroft 1/1/55
Bath Green Park 20/4/55
Millhouses 13/8/55
Leeds Holbeck 4/2/56
Millhouses 10/3/56
Grimesthorpe 4/1/59
Canklow 9/4/61
Nine Elms 2/12/62

Withdrawn 9/64

73075

To traffic 22/4/55

Works
2/11/55-3/11/55**NC**	St.Rollox
7/3/57-30/3/57**LI**	St.Rollox
24/6/59-16/7/59**GO**	Cowlairs
4/7/60-6/8/60**LC**	Cowlairs
4/6/62-11/7/62**HI**	Cowlairs

Tender
BR1C no.1201 from new

Shed
Polmadie 14/5/55

Withdrawn 12/65

73076

To traffic 29/4/55

Works
10/10/55-15/10/55**LC[TO]**	St.Rollox
16/12/55-22/12/55**LC**	St.Rollox
18/1/56-21/1/56**LC[TO]**	S.Rollox
25/6/56-28/6/56**NC[EO]**	St.Rollox
21/11/57-13/12/57**LI**	St.Rollox
25/11/59-19/12/59**GO**	Cowlairs
20/10/60-3/11/60**LC[EO]**	Cowlairs
31/10/62-24/11/62**HI**	Cowlairs
15/10/63-16/10/63**NC[EO]**	Cowlairs
30/10/63**NC[EO]**	Cowlairs

Tenders
BR1C no.1202 from new
BR1C no.1208 on 16/2/64

Shed
Polmadie 14/5/55

Withdrawn 13/7/64

73077

To traffic 13/5/55

Works
27/6/56 **NC[EO]**	St.Rollox
5/11/56 **NC[TO]**	St.Rollox
18/3/57-5/4/57 **LI**	St.Rollox
15/8/58-6/9/58 **LI**	St.Rollox
24/2/59-4/3/59 **NC[EO]**	St.Rollox
5/6/59-10/6/59 **GO**	St.Rollox
23/3/60-30/4/60 **GO**	Cowlairs
12/4/61-5/4/61 **NC**	Cowlairs
5/6/61-10/6/61 **LC**	Cowlairs
31/8/61-1/9/61 **NC[EO]**	Cowlairs
13/2/63-9/3/63 **LI**	Cowlairs
18/4/63-19/4/63 **NC[EO]**	Cowlairs
20/6/63-22/6/63 **NC[EO]**	Cowlairs
13/11/63-16/11/63 **LC[EO]**	Cowlairs
31/7/64-14/8/64 **LC[EO]**	Cowlairs
11/11/64-14/11/64 **NC[EO]**	Cowlairs

Tender
BR1C no.1203 from new

Sheds
Eastfield 9/7/55
Corkerhill 31/12/62

Withdrawn 30/12/64

Eastfield's 73077 heads K2 2-6-0 61776 at Bridge of Orchy with the 2.56pm Fort William-Glasgow, 14 September 1957; fireman on train engine leaning out with the staff. The scorch on the smokebox door suggests that the self-cleaning gear has been surreptitiously removed. J.L. Stevenson, courtesy Hamish Stevenson.

73078 and K2 61794 LOCH OICH at Crianlarich on 8 August 1959, with the 4.30pm Glasgow-Mallaig. 73078 has AWS but the conduit, bizarrely, is tacked on to the *outside* of the running plate, taking an awkward diversion for instance, to avoid the lubricator. There were one or two others like this. J.L. Stevenson, courtesy Hamish Stevenson.

73078

To traffic 13/5/55

Works
20/12/55-28/12/55**LC**	St.Rollox
15/2/56-16/2/56**NC**	St.Rollox
4/7/56**NC**	St.Rollox
23/10/56**NC**	St.Rollox
9/5/57-25/5/57**LI**	St.Rollox
24/3/58-27/3/58**LC[EO]**	Cowlairs
5/7/58-7/7/58**NC[EO]**	Cowlairs
14/10/58-5/11/58**HI**	Cowlairs
23/2/59-4/3/59**NC[EO]**	St.Rollox
25/8/59-17/9/59**LC**	Cowlairs
17/12/59-30/1/60**GO**	Cowlairs
30/11/60-3/12/60**LC[EO]**	Cowlairs
4/7/61-13/7/61**LC**	Cowlairs
27/11/61-1/12/61**LC[EO]**	Cowlairs
17/9/62-20/10/62**LI**	Cowlairs
28/3/63-30/3/63**NC[EO]**	Cowlairs

Tender
BR1C no.1204 from new

Sheds
Eastfield 9/7/55
Carstairs 29/1/66

Withdrawn 14/7/66

73079

To traffic 31/5/55

Works
30/11/56-21/12/56**LC**	St.Rollox
10/9/57-12/10/57**LI**	St.Rollox
12/5/58-31/5/58**LC[EO]**	Cowlairs
10/8/59-3/9/59**HC[EO]**	Cowlairs
9/4/60-30/4/60**HC**	Cowlairs
21/2/61-22/4/61**GO**	Cowlairs
7/6/62-29/6/62**LC**	Cowlairs
1/8/63-31/8/63**HI**	Cowlairs
19/7/64-7/8/64**NC[EO]**	Cowlairs
30/11/64-26/12/64**LC[EO]**	Cowlairs
24/5/66-10/6/66**LC**	Cowlairs

Tenders
BR1C no.1205 from new
BR1B no.1306 on 26/2/65

Sheds
Corkerhill 9/7/55
Polmadie 22/4/67

Withdrawn 1/5/67

A minor freight for 73079, passing Bellahouston station on 18 April 1964. An interesting load; three opens with barrels, a van and a mineral. J.L. Stevenson, courtesy Hamish Stevenson.

73080

To traffic 6/55
Works
10/3/58-12/4/58**LI-HI** 120,182 Eastleigh
Piston rod packing renewed and modified
Isolating cock pipes and equipment fitted
Briquette container changed and modified
Blowdown valve operating gear modified
R5900 Safety chains between engine and tender
Smokebox diaphragm chains fitted
T2263 Piston rod packing [renewed and modified]
28/5/59-12/6/59**NC** 174,812 Ashford
4983 ATC equipment
21/9/60-1/10/60**LC** 208,147 Eastleigh
30/12/60-4/2/61**GO** 213,641 Eastleigh
Nameplates MERLIN fitted w/e 4/2/61
24/2/64-11/4/64**LI-HI** Eastleigh

Boilers
No.1495 from new
No.1500 4/2/61

Tender
BR1B no.1206 from new

Sheds
Stewarts Lane 21/6/55
Nine Elms 14/6/59
Weymouth 26/11/59
Eastleigh 18/3/61
Weymouth 3/5/61

Withdrawn 12/66

73080 MERLIN at Nine Elms, on the coaling roads, 10 September 1966. This is one of those curious instances brought about by 73080 obtaining a replacement section at the front of the running plate. On the far side the steps are 'originals' as bolted on at Derby; the nearest steps are higher, meaning that the section of running plate was originally on a Doncaster-built example. Peter Groom.

73081

To traffic 17/6/55

Works
5/12/55-19/1/56 **LC**	Crewe
14/9/56-20/10/56**LI**	44,825 Eastleigh T2263 Piston rod packing renewed
23/10/57-9/11/57**LI**	89,911 Eastleigh
13/3/59-11/4/59**LI-HI**	153,339 Eastleigh
	Draught screens
	4983 ATC gear Injector overflow pipes
	T2263 Piston rod packing [R]
9/1/61-11/2/61**GO**	223,403 Eastleigh
	Nameplates EXCALIBUR fitted w/e 11/2/61
	634 monel metal stays renewed 701 nuts renewed
	151 new small tubes 'Tube Products'
	2 fusible plugs
5/12/62-18/12/62**LC**	72,274 Eastleigh
7/11/63-14/12/63**LI**	103,290 Eastleigh
	430 monel metal stays riveted over 430 nuts renewed
	48 studs and seams repaired 2 fusible plugs

Boiler
No.1620 7/11/61

Tender
BR1B no.1207 from new

Sheds
Stewarts Lane 7/7/55
Nine Elms 14/6/59
Guildford 8/6/65

Withdrawn 7/66

73081 EXCALIBUR heading west from Brockenhurst at Lymington Junction, 14 September 1963. The signalbox is behind us here; the Lymington branch is going off under the very wheels of the Class 5. Stephen Gradidge.

A Stewarts Lane Class 5, 73081, comes into Ashford on 1 August 1959. Its transfer to Nine Elms, following electrification on its home ground is officially recorded as June 1959 but it clearly stayed on the Eastern Section till the general abolition of steam later in the year. On the left is an N mogul, Redhill's 31817. Stephen Gradidge.

73082

To traffic 24/6/55

Works
28/12/55-17/2/56**LC** — Crewe
28/10/57-30/11/57**LI-HI** — 95,815 Eastleigh
H.O.9216 Blowdown valve gear
Piston head ring grooves deepened
R5900 Safety links between engine and tender
T2263 Piston rod packing [O]
28/7/59-15/8/59**LI** — 165,514 Eastleigh
Injector overflow pipes and brackets
Isolating cock
Nameplates CAMELOT fitted w/e 15/8/59
T2263 Piston rod packing [U]
4/3/60-19/3/60**LC** — 184,858 Eastleigh
5/12/60-24/12/60**LC** — 212,988 Eastleigh
1/8/61-2/9/62**GO** — 236,978 Eastleigh
T2291 Modification of tender coal hole door plates for improved access
15/11/63-21/12/63**LI** — 88,519 Eastleigh
ATC equipment made operative

Tender
BR1B no.1208 from new

Sheds
Stewarts Lane 7/7/55
Nine Elms 14/6/59
Guildford 8/6/65

Withdrawn 6/66, preserved on the Bluebell Railway.

73082 CAMELOT, another former Stewarts Lane Class 5, at new home shed Nine Elms, 19 September 1959; short reach rod, yellow circle under cabside number indicating water treatment. Stephen Gradidge.

CAMELOT at Alton on Sunday 2 October 1960; the train, a Southampton Docks-Waterloo 'boat', had been re-routed owing to PW work on the main line. B.H. Kimber.

73083

To traffic 7/55

Works
30/7/57-17/8/57**LI-HI**	105,403 Eastleigh
	T2263 [overhauled and modified]
	T2291 Modification of tender coal hole doors for improved access
15/11/57-14/12/57**LC-HC**	114,584 Eastleigh
14/9/59-10/10/59**GO**	182,549 Eastleigh
	5548 Hinged cab windows T2263 T2272 T2291
	Injector overflow pipes
	Steam brake pipes
	Isolating cock
	4983 ATC equipment
	E3329 Modified pistons for continuous blowdown valves
	Handwritten on BR9637 form = "nameplate fitted PENDRAGON per E,leigh 16/10/59"
6/3/62-31/3/62**LI**	93,778 Eastleigh
16/10/62-3/11/62**NC-LC**	111,389 Eastleigh
9/6/64-2/7/64**LC-HC**	Eastleigh

Boilers
No.1606 from new
No.1168 10/10/59

Tender
BR1B no.1209 from new

Sheds
Stewarts Lane 7/7/55
Nine Elms 14/6/59
Feltham 14/9/64
Weymouth 20/11/64

Withdrawn 9/66

In appalling external condition, 73083 (formerly PENDRAGON) has found its way to Oxford (doubtless on an inter-Regional working) from its Weymouth home on 15 May 1965. It looks bad enough to be on its way to the scrapyard but like most steam locomotives worked perfectly happily despite the grime. It survived for over a year, to September 1966. AWS battery box under cab. Stephen Gradidge.

73084

To traffic 29/7/55

Works
8/10/56-24/10/56**NC**	Derby
28/5/57-8/6/57**NC**	80,731 Eastleigh
23/9/57-12/10/57**LI**	87,997 Eastleigh
6/1/58-11/1/58**NC**	100,098 Eastleigh
	R5900 Safety chains between engine and tender
	T2263 Piston rod packing
	T2272 Piston heads [U]
30/9/59-31/10/59**GO**	171,214 Eastleigh
	T2263 Piston rod packing [part renewed]
	T2272 Piston heads [Renewed 3 ring type]
	4983 ATC equipment
	Injector overflow pipes Isolating cock
	5548 Hinged windows cab front
	Steam brake pipes
	Blowdown valves operating gear
	Nameplates TINTAGEL fitted w/e 31/10/59
15/2/62-17/3/62**LI**	97,599 Eastleigh
	T2291 Tender coal hole door plates modified for improved access
	578 monel metal stays riveted over 578 nuts renewed
	30 new small tubes 'Stewart and Lloyds'
	Seams and studs recaulked 2 fusible plugs
28/9/64-30/10/64**LC**	Eastleigh
5/8/65-9/8/65**LC**	Eastleigh

Boilers
No.1499 from new
No.1012 31/10/59

Tender
BR1B no.1210 from new

Sheds
Stewarts Lane 7/7/55
Nine Elms 14/6/59
Feltham 25/10/65
Eastleigh 24/10/65

Withdrawn 12/65

In dire state, though doubtless in fine fettle mechanically, 73084 stands outside the 'new shed' at Nine Elms on 16 October 1965, the TINTAGEL plates stored or sold; few British locomotives could have carried names for such a brief time. 73084 managed brief transfers (whether actual or not is unclear) to Feltham and Eastleigh before being withdrawn at the end of the year. Stephen Gradidge.

73085

To traffic 5/8/55

Works
15/11/56-10/12/56**NC**	Derby
31/12/57-18/1/58**LI-HI**	108,784 Eastleigh
	R5900 Safety links between engine and tender,
	HO9216 Manual blowdown valves gear modified
	Briquette tube feeder modified, 1" wide piston rod packing,
	P.P. compression springs HO9089 pipework modified for access
	to washout plug. T2262 'Klinger' steam valve pistons [renewed 1" wide]
27/4/59-15/5/59**NC**	171,201 Ashford
	4983 ATC equipment
	Draught screens
2/7/59-8/8/59**NC-LC**	172,830 Eastleigh
	Isolating cock, Injector overflow pipes and brackets
	Nameplates MELISANDE fitted
	T2263 Piston rod packing [U]
	Release delayed due to annual works holiday
23/8/60-17/9/60**GO**	213,190 Eastleigh
	Injector overflow pipes,
	T2081 regulator valve stainless steel no.2 [new test] valve ex.73052
4/5/62-12/5/62**LC**	65,990 Eastleigh
	T2081 regulator valve, stainless steel [U]
27/9/62-3/11/62**NC-LC**	80,892 Eastleigh
	T2081 [U]
18/12/63-4/1/64**LC**	123,353 Eastleigh
27/5/64-25/6/64**LC-HC**	Eastleigh
20/5/65-25/6/65**LI**	Eastleigh
7/12/65-16/12/65**LC**	Eastleigh
16/5/66-19/5/66**LC**	Eastleigh
19/12/66-20/12/66**NC**	Eastleigh

Tender
BR1B no.1211 from new

Sheds
Stewarts Lane 7/7/55
Nine Elms 14/6/59
Feltham 28/8/65
Eastleigh 22/11/65
Nine Elms 27/6/66

Withdrawn 7/7/67

73085 at Nine Elms the same day, 16 October 1965. Interestingly, it has picked up one of the big 1F tenders, obviously from one withdrawn in the 73110-73119 series. Again, *sans* nameplate. Stephen Gradidge.

73086

To traffic 16/8/55

Works
1/2/57-13/2/57**C**	Derby
4/9/57-21/9/57**LI-HI**	99,028 Eastleigh
18/12/57-11/1/58**LC-HC**	110,069 Eastleigh
	R5900 Safety chains between engine and tender
	Pipework in cab
	T2263 Piston rod packing
	T2272 Piston heads [U]
11/11/59-12/12/59**GO**	191,066 Eastleigh 4983 ATC equipment Speedometer gear
	Isolating cock Blowdown valve operating gear Injector overflow pipes
	5548 Hinged cab windows Steam brake pipes
	Nameplates THE GREEN KNIGHT fitted w/e 12/12/59
8/7/60-9/7/60**LC**	18,942 Eastleigh T2263 Piston rod packing [U] T2272 Piston heads [U]
16/5/61-7/6/61**NC-LC**	48,715 Eastleigh

Boilers
No.1501 from new
No.1499 12/12/59

Tender
BR1B no.1212 from new

Sheds
Stewarts Lane 7/7/55
Nine Elms 14/6/59

Withdrawn 10/66

73086 THE GREEN KNIGHT at Nine Elms, 5 May 1960; short reach rod, AWS and new-type 'bell' whistle instead of the original chime, which suffered deterioration over the years. The temporary plate on the cabside (other Regions did this too) indicates that the good knight is subject to some modification/test. Peter Groom.

73087

To traffic 26/8/55

Works

	W/E 7/7/56 tablet catching gear fitted not booked into works
	To 71G Bath [Green Park] for Somerset and Dorset
18/1/57-2/2/57**LC**	Eastleigh
6/6/57-17/6/57**NC**	Derby
9/10/57-26/10/57**LI**	81,648 Eastleigh
20/1/59-7/2/59**LI-HI**	140,167 Eastleigh
	T2263 Piston rod packing
	T2272 Piston heads
26/2/59-28/2/59**NC**	141,972 Eastleigh
	4983 ATC equipment
	T2263 and T2272 both [U]
21/4/61-27/5/61**GO**	208,906 Eastleigh
	T2291 1ender coalhole door plates modified for improved access
	Nameplates LINETTE fitted w/e 27/5/61
	Flange patches electrically copper welded
6/3/64-18/4/64**LI-HI**	Eastleigh
	367 monel metal stays riveted over 367 nuts renewed
	Foundation Ring 28 rivets repaired

Boilers
No.1502 from new
No.1630 27/5/61

Tender
BR1B no.1213 from new

Sheds
Stewarts Lane 7/7/55
Bath Green Park 27/8/56
Eastleigh 27/10/56
Bath Green Park 19/7/57
Stewarts Lane 8/10/57
Bath Green Park 17/5/58
Nie Elms 13/10/58
Bath Green Park 13/6/59
Nine Elms 5/4/60
Bath Green Park 18/6/60
Nine Elms 24/9/60
Bath Green Park 17/6/61
Nine Elms 23/8/61
Feltham 14/9/64
Eastleigh 12/10/64
Guildford 8/6/65

Withdrawn 10/66

73088

To traffic 1/9/55

Works

26/2/57-19/3/57**LI**	Derby
24/9/57-4/10/57**NC**	90,951 Eastleigh
20/11/57-7/12/57**LC**	93,606 Eastleigh
11/12/58-3/1/59**LC**	136,825 Eastleigh
	T2263 Piston rod packing [U]
	T2272 Piston heads [U]
	T2298 BR standard firebars [U]
25/2/59-7/3/59**NC-LC**	139,063 Eastleigh
	T2263 T2272 T2298 [U]
	4983 ATC equipment
26/5/60-18/6/60**LC**	189,407 Eastleigh
	Tread plates
	T2263 and T2272 both [U] T2298 cancelled
28/3/61-6/5/61**GO**	212,632 Eastleigh
	Heavy boiler repairs Draught screens
	Blowdown gear
	T2291 Tender coalhole door plates modified for improved access
	W/E 6/5/61 nameplates JOYOUS GARD fitted
	2 fusible plugs
26/7/62-28/7/62**NC**	42,375 Eastleigh
9/4/64-15/4/64**LI-HI**	Eastleigh
	436 monel metal studs riveted over 436 nuts renewed
	14 new small tubes 'Stewart and Lloyds'
	2 fusible plugs
18/8/65-17/9/65**LC**	Eastleigh

Boilers
No.1503 from new
No.863 6/5/61

Tender
BR1B no.1214 from new

Sheds
Stewarts Lane 7/7/55
Bath Green Park 17/5/58
Nine Elms 13/10/58
Guildford 25/10/65

Withdrawn 10/66

73089

To traffic 9/9/55

Works
5/4/57-2/5/57**LC**	Derby
17/10/57-9/11/57**LI**	104,374 Eastleigh
26/11/58-6/12/58**LC**	154,642 Eastleigh T2263 Piston rod packing [U]
15/4/59-2/5/59**NC-LC**	168,369 Eastleigh
	T2263 Piston rod packing [U]
	4983 ATC equipment
	Nameplates MAID OF ASTOLAT fitted w/e 30/5/59
13/4/60-4/6/60**GO**	206,586 Eastleigh
	T2263 [R], Tread plates
	Injector overflow pipes
	Cab windows and screens
	Steam brake pipes
	52 rivets renewed with studs 2 fusible plugs
11/9/62-29/9/62**LI**	100,057 Eastleigh
	395 monel metal stays riveted over 395 nuts renewed
	30 new small tubes 'Stewart and Lloyds'
13/5/64-10/6/64**LC-HC**	Eastleigh

Boilers
No.1504 from new
No.997 4/6/60

Tender
BR1B no.1215 from new

Sheds
Stewarts Lane 7/7/55
Nine Elms 6/6/58
Eastleigh 14/9/64
Guildford 25/10/65

Withdrawn 9/66

A pleasing side view of 73089 MAID OF ASTOLAT at Eastleigh on 18 September 1960; 'bell'-type whistle by the look of it. Stephen Gradidge.

73090

To traffic 7/10/55

Works
12/11/57-11/12/57**LI**	82,494 Derby
	R5900 Safety links between engine and tender
	R6132 Fit protection shields
	333 Stayhead nuts renewed 60 new small tubes
9/6/58-26/6/58**NC[EO]**	18,491 Derby
9/60	Doncaster BR Green livery
7/7/63**C**	Derby
2/9/63-4/10/63**C**	Crewe

Annual mileage
1955 9,948
1956 41,782
1957 31,836

Boiler
No.1505 from new
No.1612 13/8/60

Tenders
BR1C no.1272 from new
BR1C no.1274

Sheds
Patricroft 8/10/55
Shrewsbury 6/9/58
Oxley 23/1/65
Shrewsbury 6/3/65

Withdrawn 9/10/65

73091

To traffic 14/10/55

Works
8/11/55-11/11/55**NC[EO,Rect]**	2,887 Derby
	Ashpan
28/8/56-1/9/56**NC[TO]**	38,429 Derby
	Tender tank
10/4/57-11/4/57**LC[TO]**	58,882 Derby
23/9/57-3/10/57**LC**	73,581 Derby
	MDL/1320 Piston valve liners with increased number of ports
14/2/58-6/3/58**LI**	88,831 Derby
	R5900 Safety links between engine and tender
10/2/59-24/2/59**LC**	Wolverhampton
5/60	Doncaster BR Green livery

Annual mileage
1955 9,306
1956 41,093
1957 33,132

Boilers
No.1506 from new
No.838 27/5/60

Tender
BR1C no.1273 from new

Sheds
Patricroft 5/11/55
Shrewsbury 6/9/58
Gloucester [Barnwood] 7/10/61
Gloucester [Horton Road] 4/5/64

Withdrawn 5/67

73092

To traffic 21/10/55

Works
4/11/57	MDL/1320 piston valve liners with increased number of ports
5/2/58-24/2/58LI	95,084 Derby E5900 Safety links between engine and tender
5/60	Doncaster BR Green livery

Annual mileage
1955 8,242
1956 42,837
1957 41,080

Boiler
No.1609 from new

Tenders
BR1C no.1274 from new
BR1C no.1272

Sheds
Patricroft 5/11/55
Shrewsbury 6/9/58
Gloucester [Barnwood] 7/10/61
Gloucester [Horton Road] 4/5/64
Bath Green Park 20/7/64
Eastleigh 12/4/65
Guildford 25/10/65

Withdrawn 7/7/67

73092 at Eastleigh on 5 September 1965; whistle now disappeared from its hitherto familiar and prominent site behind the chimney. This came about with 73100 onwards from Doncaster and the earlier-numbered but later-built 73090 from Derby. It is 1965 and of course the loco could hardly be filthier. Stephen Gradidge.

73093

To traffic 4/11/55

Works
8/11/55	MDL/1320 Piston valve liners with increased number of ports
26/11/57-19/12/57**LI**	90,814 Derby
	R5900 Safety links between engine and tender
	R6132 Fit protection shields
2/9/58-25/9/58**LC**	26,430 Derby
12/10/59-7/11/59**LC**	Shrewsbury
7/3/60-10/5/60**HI**	Wolverhampton BR Green livery

Annual mileage
1955 5,816
1956 41,582
1957 43,586

Boilers
No.1610 from new
No.1760 27/4/65

Tender
BR1C no.1275 from new

Sheds
Patricroft 5/11/55
Shrewsbury 6/9/58
Gloucester [Barnwood] 7/10/61
Gloucester [Horton Road] 4/5/64
Bath Green Park 7/3/65
Eastleigh 12/4/65
Guildford 25/10/65

Withdrawn 7/7/67

73094

To traffic 10/11/55

Works
21/5/57-6/6/57**LC**	63,516 Derby
	MDL/1320 Piston valve liners with increased number of ports
25/2/58-25/3/58**HI**	89,827 Derby
8/1/60-5/2/60**LC**	Wolverhampton
29/9/60-3/11/60**I**	Doncaster BR Green livery
6/8/64-23/9/64**LI-HC**	Eastleigh WR loco. W/E 12/9/64 awaiting material from Swindon
	430 monel metal stays riveted over 430 nuts renewed
	151 new small tubes 'Stewart and Lloyds'

Annual mileage
1955 6,467
1956 43,089
1957 37,129

Boiler
No.1611 from new

Tender
BR1C no.1276 from new

Sheds
Patricroft 3/12/55
Shrewsbury 6/9/58
Bristol Barrow Road 7/10/61
Gloucester [Barnwood] 2/12/61
Shrewsbury 25/5/64
Patricroft 18/7/65

Withdrawn 13/5/67

One prepared earlier; 73094 new at Derby on 12 November 1955 with 1C tender, its two plates showing very clearly. After a while these would be permanently invisible. R.J. Buckley, Initial Photographics.

73095

To traffic 17/11/55

Works
8/7/57-15/8/57**LI**	72,819 Derby
7/60	Doncaster BR Green livery

Annual mileage
1955 4,888
1956 45,106
1957 38,763

Boilers
No.1612 from new
No.1506 14/7/60
No.1793 18/7/62

Tender
BR1C no.1277 from new

Sheds
Patricroft 17/11/55
Shrewsbury 6/9/58
Croes Newydd 28/8/65
Agecroft 30/4/66

Withdrawn 27/8/66

73096

To traffic 25/11/55

Works
13/3/56-15/3/56**NC**	12,080 Derby
2/6/57-7/6/57**LC[TO]**	62,734 Derby
19/3/58-14/4/58**LI**	96,812 Derby
	R5900 Safety links between engine and tender
19/11/59-31/12/59**LC**	Wolverhampton BR Green livery
	90 copper stays riveted over 1,612 nuts renewed
	151 new small tubes
9/2/61-24/3/61**GO**	Doncaster
26/8/63-2/10/63**LI**	Crewe

Annual mileage
1955 4,032
1956 45,506
1957 38,464

Boilers
No.1613 from new
No.1610 24/3/61

Tender
BR1C no.1278 from new

Sheds
Patricroft 3/12/55
Shrewsbury 6/9/58
Gloucester [Barnwood] 18/6/62
Gloucester [Horton Road] 4/5/64
Oxley 7/11/64
Nuneaton 6/3/65
Croes Newydd 19/6/65
Patricroft 24/7/65

Withdrawn 25/11/67, preserved on the Mid Hants Railway

Under the wires at Crewe South on 21 April 1963 as Shrewsbury's 73095 rumbles by light to the shed. It is interesting to note that it has less than its proper quota of electrification flashes – one on the firebox maybe but where are all the ones at the front? Stephen Gradidge.

73096 at the little terminus at Windermere, 31 July 1967, on the 11am to Euston; these were the last days of seaside and other holiday towns enjoying summertime connections direct to the capital. Poor old 73096 is inevitably in deplorable nick, made worse by the horrible daubed 9H, Patricroft's last code. J.L. Stevenson, courtesy Hamish Stevenson.

The Book of the BR Standard Class 5 4-6-0s

73097

To traffic 6/12/55

Works
29/11/56-4/12/56**NC[EO]**	41,560 Derby
6/3/57-27/3/57**LC**	48,486 Derby
18/12/57-7/1/58**LI**	79,436 Derby
	R5900 Safety links between engine and tender
	R6132 Fit protection shield over tender leading axle
9/9/59-16/10/59**LC**	Wolverhampton BR Green livery
6/11/59-9/11/59**LC**	Wolverhampton
7/2/64-20/4/64**C**	Darlington

Annual mileage
1955 2,616
1956 40,772
1957 36,048

Boiler
No.1614 from new

Tender
BR1C no.1279 from new

Sheds
Patricroft 6/12/55
Shrewsbury 6/9/58
Patricroft 18/7/65

Withdrawn 6/5/67

73098

To traffic 15/12/55

Works
31/1/57-4/2/57**LC[TO]**	50,367 Derby
9/10/57-23/10/57**LC**	77,344 Derby
3/12/57-24/12/57**LI**	80,838 Derby
	R5900 Safety links between engine and tender
	R6132 Fit protection shield over tender leading axle
30/6/59-14/7/59**LC**	Cowlairs
28/3/60-30/4/60**NC[EO]**	Cowlairs
27/3/61-29/4/61**GO**	Cowlairs
1/2/62-17/3/62**LC**	Cowlairs
20/9/62-12/10/62**LC[TO]**	Cowlairs
13/12/62-21/12/62**NC[EO**	Cowlairs
22/8/63-19/10/63**HI**	Cowlairs
8/11/63 **NC[EO]**	Cowlairs
17/2/64-28/2/64**LC[EO]**	Cowlairs
29/9/65**NC**	Cowlairs

Annual mileage
1955 1,536
1956 46,378
1957 32,952
1958 41,265
1959 10,090

Boiler
No.1615 from new

Tenders
BR1C no.1280 from new
BR1H no.1000 26/8/65

Sheds
Patricroft 31/12/55
Chester West 4/10/58
Polmadie 22/11/58

Withdrawn 3/3/66

73099

To traffic 30/12/55

Works
14/1/58-3/2/58**LI**	86,619 Derby
	R5900 Safety links between engine and tender
	R6132 Fit protection shields
3/4/59-28/4/59**NC[EO]**	Cowlairs
15/12/59-31/12/59**LC[TO]**	St.Rollox
3/7/61-16/9/61**GO**	Cowlairs
20/6/63-3/8/63**HI**	Cowlairs
9/12/64-11/12/64**NC[EO]**	Cowlairs
21/4/65-1/5/65**LC**	Inverurie
26/5/66-10/6/66**LC**	Cowlairs
13/7/66-16/7/66**LC[EO]**	Cowlairs

Annual mileage
1955 29
1956 44,363
1957 40,444
1958 38,895
1959 8,500
[up to date of transfer to Sc.R. 22/3/59]

Boiler
No.1616 from new

Tender
BR1C no.1281 from new

Sheds
Patricroft 31/12/55
Chester West 4/10/58
Polmadie 22/11/58
Hamilton 4/7/60
Polmadie 21/10/61

Withdrawn 10/66

73099 at an unknown place, at an unknown time. It will be Scotland probably but you can never tell; 73099 was one of three sent to Polmadie from the old GW shed at Chester. Following long tradition the Polmadie Class 5s regularly made their way deep into England, to the North West in especial, but not much further south than that. Paul Chancellor Collection.

73100

To traffic 27/8/55

Works
26/6/56-4/7/56**LC**	St.Rollox
4/9/57-3/10/57**LI**	St.Rollox
29/10/57-6/11/57**NC**	St.Rollox
23/5/58-3/6/58**NC[EO]**	Cowlairs
30/6/59-4/7/59**NC[EO]**	Cowlairs
11/8/59-28/8/59**LC [EO]**	Cowlairs
17/12/59-6/2/60**GO**	Cowlairs
12/4/61-20/4/61**NC[EO]**	Cowlairs
12/4/62-4/5/62**LC[EO]**	Cowlairs
30/7/62-1/9/62**HI**	Cowlairs
29/6/64-28/8/64**LC [EO]**	Cowlairs
18/11/64-20/11/64**NC**	Cowlairs
25/2/65-1/5/65**LI**	Cowlairs
16/8/65-28/8/65**NC**	Cowlairs
25/1/66-2/2/66**NC**	Cowlairs
14/6/66-25/6/66**LC[EO]**	Cowlairs

Tenders
BR1B no.1282 from new
BR1B no.1306
BR1B no.1395 26/2/65

Shed
Corkerhill 2/9/55

Withdrawn 20/1/67

73101

To traffic 2/9/55

Works
11/10/56-7/11/56**LC[EO]**	St.Rollox
7/10/57-9/11/57**LI**	St.Rollox
27/1/59-2/3/59**LC[EO]**	Cowlairs
5/7/60-20/8/60**GO**	Cowlairs
19/1/63-23/2/63**HI**	Cowlairs
17/8/64-29/9/64**LC[EO]**	Cowlairs
16/2/65-20/2/65**NC[EO]**	Cowlairs
3/8/65-4/8/65**NC[EO]**	Cowlairs
5/1/66-29/1/66**LC[EO]**	Cowlairs
18/3/66-30/3/66**NC[EO]**	Cowlairs
24/4/66-7/5/66**NC[EO]**	Cowlairs

Tenders
BR1B no.1283 from new
BR1B no.1302
BR1B no.1285

Shed
Corkerhill 1/9/55

Withdrawn 24/8/66

73100-73104 were delivered new to Corkerhill over August-September 1955 and never left the place; all were withdrawn from there as steam was eliminated in Scotland. 73100 (whistle now placed more conventionally on the firebox top) is in the shed yard on 16 June 1957; it was a landmark in engine picking, for with this loco the higher Doncaster front steps came into the world. www.transporttreasury.co.uk

73101 with a train of oil tanks, Ardrossan-Perth, passing Polmadie on 4 May 1957; BR5 stencilled on buffer beam. J.L. Stevenson, courtesy Hamish Stevenson.

One of the Corkerhill ten, 73102, at its home shed on 14 October 1956 J.L. Stevenson, courtesy Hamish Stevenson.

73102

To traffic 14/9/55

Works
18/12/56-26/12/56**LC[EO]**	St.Rollox
11/3/57-23/3/57**LC**	St.Rollox
11/10/57-12/10/57**LC**	St.Rollox
24/10/57-15/11/57**HI**	St.Rollox
14/10/58-30/10/58**LC[EO]**	Cowlairs
3/8/59-17/8/59**LC**	Cowlairs
25/4/60-18/6/60**GO**	Cowlairs
18/2/61-11/3/61**LC[TO]**	Cowlairs
26/5/62-23/6/62**HI**	Cowlairs
31/12/64-27/2/65**LI**	Cowlairs
30/12/65-15/1/66**NC**	Cowlairs

Tenders
BR1B no.1284 from new
BR1 no.1001

Shed
Corkerhill 14/9/55

Withdrawn 31/12/66

73103

To traffic 21/9/55

Works
16/10/57**LC**	St.Rollox
30/1/58-1/3/58**LI**	Cowlairs
2/10/59-30/10/59**GO**	Cowlairs
16/4/62-18/5/62**HI**	Cowlairs
4/6/64-27/6/64**HI**	Cowlairs
19/2/65-20/2/65**NC[EO]**	Cowlairs
9/9/65-?	

Tender
BR1B no.1285 from new

Shed
Corkerhill 1/10/55

Withdrawn 22/10/65

Getting 73102 ready at Corkerhill on 5 April 1965. The withdrawal of Corkerhill's BR Class 5s would get underway that very month, with the loss of 73123. All would be gone by the end of 1966 except 73100, the first in and last out as it were. It officially staggered on to January 1967. Hamish Stevenson.

Corkerhill's 73103 at Eastfield shed after overhaul at Cowlairs, 1 March 1958. The whistle's removal to the firebox top was due to fears that it could not always be heard well enough so near to the exhaust of the chimney. J.L. Stevenson, courtesy Hamish Stevenson.

Looking good on our wonderfully busy but long-vanished railway of happier times, 73103 hurries through Bellahouston on 11 July 1964. The carriage pilot is D3277. Hamish Stevenson.

73104

To traffic 27/9/55

Works
15/2/56-17/2/56**LC[EO]**	St.Rollox
15/8/56-18/8/56**LC[EO]**	St.Rollox
12/12/57-26/12/57**LI**	St.Rollox
29/5/58-20/6/58**LC[EO]**	Cowlairs
2/7/60-**GO**	Cowlairs
12/6/63-10/7/63**HI**	Cowlairs
3/1/64-11/1/64**NC[EO]**	Cowlairs
13/11/64-12/12/64**LC[EO]**	Cowlairs
21/1/65-22/1/65**LC**	Inverurie

Tender
BR1B no.1286 from new

Shed
Corkerhill 1/10/55

Withdrawn 22/10/65

73105

To traffic 12/55

Works
24/2/58-29/3/58**LI**	Cowlairs
5/3/59-12/3/59**NC[EO]**	St.Rollox
14/9/59-8/10/59**LC[EO]**	Cowlairs
16/3/60-7/5/60**GO**	Cowlairs
11/6/62-11/8/62**HI**	Cowlairs
21/8/64-12/9/64**LC[EO]**	Cowlairs
19/2/65-27/2/65**NC[EO]**	Cowlairs
20/9/65-25/9/65**NC**	Cowlairs
26/10/65-20/11/65**LC**	Cowlairs
30/5/66-18/6/66**LC[EO]**	Cowlairs

Tender
BR1B no.1287 from new

Sheds
Eastfield 9/12/55
Grangemouth 21/12/64
Stirling 18/10/65
Corkerhill 25/6/66

Withdrawn 26/9/66

73104 with an up freight at Newton Stewart, 15 April 1963. Poor old 73104 is lamentably filthy and among various leaks is losing steam from the valve at the steam lance smokebox valve. J.L. Stevenson, courtesy Hamish Stevenson.

73105 comes into platform 3 at Carlisle under the Victoria Road bridge, double heading a Black Five on a train from – probably – Glasgow. Note the unsightly external AWS conduit, seen on 73078 earlier. D. Forsyth, Paul Chancellor Collection.

73106

To traffic 12/55

Works
30/1/56-3/2/56**NC**	St.Rollox
29/6/56**NC[EO]**	St.Rollox
9/2/57**LC[TO]**	St.Rollox
25/2/58-25/3/58**LI**	Cowlairs
20/6/58-21/6/58**NC[EO]**	Cowlairs
21/11/58-1/12/58**NC[EO]**	Cowlairs
13/2/59-28/4/59**LC[EO]**	Cowlairs
20/4/60-21/5/60**GO**	Cowlairs
26/4/61-27/4/61**NC**	Cowlairs
19/3/62-21/4/62**HI**	Cowlairs
29/1/63-9/2/63**LC[EO]**	Cowlairs
4/6/63-7/6/63**NC[EO]**	Cowlairs
3/7/63-6/7/63**NC[EO]**	Cowlairs
2/3/64-20/3/64**LC[EO]**	Cowlairs
22/8/64-4/9/64**LC[EO]**	Cowlairs
29/1/65-30/1/65**NC[EO**	Cowlairs

Tender
BR1B no.1288 from new

Sheds
Eastfield 24/12/55
Inverness 5/7/57
Perth 21/10/57
Corkerhill 1/7/64

Withdrawn 19/6/65

73107

To traffic 12/55

Works
23/12/57-8/2/58**LI**	Cowlairs
27/9/58-4/10/58**NC[EO]**	Cowlairs
8/12/58-13/12/58**NC[EO]**	Cowlairs
10/8/59-20/8/59**LC[EO]**	Cowlairs
28/9/59-7/11/59**GO**	Cowlairs
23/1/61-4/2/61**LC[EO]**	Cowlairs
30/6/61-19/8/61**LC[EO]**	Cowlairs
4/1/62-3/2/62**LC[EO]**	Cowlairs
10/4/62-1/6/62**HI**	Cowlairs
30/9/64-31/10/64**HI**	Cowlairs
19/8/65-21/8/65**NC[EO]**	Cowlairs
29/11/65-4/12/65**NC[EO]**	Cowlairs

Tender
BR1B no.1289 from new

Sheds
Eastfield 23/12/55
Inverness 5/7/57
Perth 21/10/57
Motherwell 1/7/64

Withdrawn 2/9/66

73108

To traffic 12/55

Works
28/6/56**NC[EO]**	St.Rollox
16/11/56-20/11/56**LC[EO]**	St.Rollox
22/4/58-17/5/58**LI**	Cowlairs
9/3/59-14/3/59**NC[EO]**	St.Rollox
2/7/59-4/7/59**NC[EO]**	Cowlairs
15/9/59-16/9/59**NC[EO]**	Cowlairs
21/9/59-23/9/59**NC[EO]**	Cowlairs
13/4/60-14/4/60**NC[EO]**	Cowlairs
5/5/60-7/5/60**NC[EO]**	Cowlairs
22/6/60-6/8/60**GO**	Cowlairs
21/6/61-23/6/61**NC[EO]**	Cowlairs
8/8/61**NC[EO]**	Cowlairs
28/9/61-7/10/61**LC[EO]**	Cowlairs
3/4/63-2/5/63**HI**	Cowlairs
25/12/65-18/1/66**NC**	Cowlairs
13/7/66-16/7/66**LC[EO]**	Cowlairs

Tender
BR1B no.1290 from new

Sheds
Eastfield 21/1/56
Carstairs 29/1/66

Withdrawn 31/12/66

A beautiful sight on the turntable at Haymarket shed, 10 June 1956; the Standards, apart from the smallest 2-6-0s, probably looked better with the high sided tenders – in this case the BR1B of 7 tons and 4,725 gallons capacity. The high running plates, so prominent on the Class 5s and other Standards, were carried on the boiler not the main frame, apart from the sloping section. There, it was thought, they would be free of vibration, which would eventually make them work loose. J. Robertson, www.transporttreasury.co.uk

73109

To traffic 12/55

Works
30/1/57-6/2/57**LC[EO]**	St.Rollox
9/1/58-1/2/58**LI**	Cowlairs
18/3/59-24/3/59**NC[EO]**	St.Rollox
16/2/60-26/3/60**GO**	Cowlairs
10/5/62-2/6/62**LI**	Cowlairs
30/1/63-31/3/63**NC[EO]**	Cowlairs

Tender
BR1B no.1291 from new

Shed
Eastfield 21/1/56

Withdrawn 31/10/64

Above. Eastfield's 73109, on the coaling road on 27 May 1956. A. Battson, www.transporttreasury.co.uk

73110

To traffic 24/9/55

Works
30/9/57-19/10/57**LI-HI**	90,043 Eastleigh H.O.9216 Blow off valve and operation gear
	360 monel metal stays riveted over 360 nuts renewed
	30 new small tubes 'Howell' 2 fusible plugs
21/12/59-23/1/60**GO**	173,165 Eastleigh
	T2263 Piston rod packing [R]
	T2272 Piston heads [R]
	T2299 Smokebox door stop chains[O]
	Draught screens
	4983 ATC equipment
	Blowdown gear
	Nameplates THE RED KNIGHT fitted
2/11/60-19/11/60**LC**	31,260 Eastleigh
5/10/61-25/10/61**LC-NC**	64,294 Eastleigh
26/10/62-1/12/62**LI**	104,410 Eastleigh
	SR type fusible plugs
22/5/63-29/5/63**NC-LC**	119,943 Eastleigh
10/9/63-14/9/63**LC-NC**	126,216 Eastleigh
21/2/64-14/3/64**LC-HC**	Eastleigh
14/10/64-15/10/64**NC**	Eastleigh
28/3/66-31/3/66**NC**	Eastleigh

Boilers
No.1619 from new
No.1501 23/1/60

Tenders
BR1F no.1292 from new
BR1B no.1208

Sheds
Nine Elms 10/10/55
Eastleigh 14/9/64
Guildford 25/10/65

Withdrawn 1/67

Almost as far from Eastfield as it is possible to be (in its way an illustration of the principles behind the BR Standards) is 73110 THE RED KNIGHT at Eastleigh; big 1F tender. Les Elsey.

Its appearance sadly diminished by layers of dirt and grime and with nameplates gone, 73110 stands at Salisbury shed on 10 August 1966. J.L. Stevenson, courtesy Hamish Stevenson.

73111

To traffic 15/10/55

Works
25/5/56-21/6/56**NC-LC**	24,754 Brighton
	Casing backplate bushed and welded
24/1/58-15/2/58**LI-HI**	102,481 Eastleigh
	Briquette tube feeder modified
	Blowdown operating gear
	Piston rod packing and springs,
	Cab pipes for access to washout plugs
	T2299 Smokebox door and diaphragm chains
	330 monel metal stays riveted over 330 nuts renewed
	30 new small tubes 'Howell'
15/5/58-19/6/58**LC**	132,888 Eastleigh
	T2263 Piston rod packing
	T2299 Smoke door stop chains [U]
	W/E 14/6/58 Fabrication of tender brake shaft brackets
4/8/59-5/9/59**NC-LC**	168,896 Ashford
	4983 ATC equipment
	Draught screens
20/10/60-26/11/60**GO**	236,066 Eastleigh
	W/E 11/2/61 nameplates KING UTHER fitted at Nine Elms shed
	151 new small tubes 'Phoenix'
	2 insert patches to both copper tubeplate and copper back plate electric copper welded
3/5/61-19/5/61**LC**	10,755 Eastleigh
6/2/63-9/3/63**LI**	69,021 Eastleigh
	30 new small tubes 'Stewart and Lloyds'
6/6/63-22/6/63**LI-NC**	72,373 Eastleigh
28/10/63-16/11/63**NC-LC**	84,901 Eastleigh
12/2/64-29/2/64**NC-LC**	85,576 Eastleigh
5/5/65-13/6/65**LC**	Eastleigh
22/6/65-25/6/65**LC**	Eastleigh

Boilers
No.1620 from new
No.1624 23/11/60

Tender
BR1F no.1293 from new

Sheds
Nine Elms 10/10/55
Eastleigh 14/9/64

Withdrawn 10/65

73112

To traffic 22/10/55

Works
3/9/56-28/9/56**NC**	38,147 Brighton
9/12/57-4/1/58**LI**	96,004 Eastleigh
	H.O. UK piston rod packing
	Blowdown operating gear, pipework modified
	274 monel metal stays riveted over 280 nuts renewed
	151 new small tubes 'Stewart and Lloyds'
30/4/59-8/5/59**NC**	64,690 Eastleigh
	T2263 Piston rod packing [U]
	T2299 Smokebox door stop chains [U]
	4983 ATC equipment
4/3/60-2/4/60**GO**	199,973 Eastleigh
	T2263[R] T2299 [Refitted],
	Isolating cock
	Nameplates MORGAN LE FAY fitted cab front injector overflow pipes Steam brake pipes
	Windows and screens
16/5/61-18/5/61**LC**	46,239 Eastleigh
27/12/62-26/1/63**LI**	111,251 Eastleigh

Boiler
No.1621 from new

Tender
BR1F no.1294 from new

Sheds
Nine Elms 10/10/55
Eastleigh 14/9/64
Nine Elms 12/10/64

Withdrawn 6/65

The Book of the BR Standard Class 5 4-6-0s

73113

To traffic 10/55

Works
23/4/56-24/5/56**LC**	21,069 Brighton
	T2272 New piston heads fitted
	Washout plug bushes etc to Drg.SL/BR/1461.A.1
11/11/57-30/11/57**LI-HI**	95,985 Eastleigh
	151 new small tubes 'Stewart and Lloyds'
24/11/59-12/12/59**LI**	188,586 Eastleigh
	4983 ATC equipment
	Injector overflow pipes
	Isolating cock
	5548 Hinged cab windows
	Screens and steam brake pipes
	Nameplates LYONESSE fitted W/C 12/12/59
	T2263 piston rod packing [R]
	T2299 Smokebox door stop chains [O]
	570 monel metal stays riveted over 570 nuts renewed
22/12/60-7/1/61**NC-LC**	229,549 Eastleigh
21/11/61-20/1/62**GO**	266,431 Eastleigh
	Tender coal hole door plates modified for improved access
	Washout plugs and pipework mod
	Cab lifting brackets fitted
	W/E 23/12/61 awaiting boiler

Boiler
No.1622 from new

Tender
BR1F no.1295 from new

Sheds
Nine Elms 10/10/55
Eastleigh 14/9/64
Weymouth 25/10/65

Withdrawn 1/67

73111 KING UTHER at Clapham Junction, 16 March 1961. Stephen Gradidge.

73114

[No card in National Archive]

To traffic 11/55

Works
10/12/56**NC**	Brighton
20/2/58-15/3/58**LI-HI**	104,889 Eastleigh
	Blowdown operating gear Piston rod packing
	Briquette container modified,
	T2263 Piston rod packing [renewed] and modified]
	T2299 Smokebox door stop chains
	201 monel metal riveted over 201 nuts renewed
	31 new small tubes 'Howell'
	Foundation Ring 32 rivets repaired
3/7/59-25/7/59**NC**	176,643 Ashford
16/2/60-19/3/60**GO**	196,946 Eastleigh
	T2263 [R] T2299 [Examined]
	Nameplates ETARRE fitted
	Injector overflow pipes Draught screens, Isolating cock
	Steam brake pipes Speedometer gear Cab front
2/1/61-28/1/61**LC**	33,686 Eastleigh
26/11/62-6/12/62**LC**	105,020 Eastleigh
27/4/64-30/5/64**LI-HI**	Eastleigh 370 monel metal stays riveted over 370 nuts renewed
	34 studs and seams caulked 2 fusible plugs

Boilers
No.1623 from new
No.1629 19/3/60

Tender
BR1F no.1296 from new

Sheds
Nine Elms 10/10/55
Eastleigh 14/9/64
Weymouth 25/10/65

Withdrawn 6/66

A dirty 73114 at Basingstoke, 20 June 1956. It had earlier in the year been loaned to the Western Region, from February to April, as the Region's contribution to the shortage of Kings, following their bogie problems. The LMR, for instance, sent some Pacifics. The Southern sent four of its BR Class 5s as well as 73114; 73085, 73088, 73110 and 73117. 73085 and 73086 were from Stewarts Lane, the other three from Nine Elms; all were back on the Southern by April. Stephen Gradidge.

73114 at Nine Elms, 21 September 1957; nameplate as yet some way off. H15 30487 shows its smiling face; behind is a T9. Stephen Gradidge.

73115

To traffic 15/11/55

Works
6/7/56-9/8/56**NC-LC**	25,574 Brighton
	Casing top sides and back plate washout holes bushed and new plugs inserted
13/12/57-11/1/58**LI-HI**	90,548 Eastleigh
	H.O.8895 UK piston rod packing Pipework in cab
	Briquette tube feeder modified
	Blowdown valve and operating gear
	151 new small tubes 'Howell'
	Foundation ring 32 rivets repaired
23/10/59-13/11/59**NC**	177,101 Ashford
	4983 ATC equipment
5/1/60-30/1/60**GO**	184,080 Eastleigh
	T2263 Piston rod packing [R]
	T2272 Piston heads 3 ring [R]
	T2299 Smokebox door stop chains[O]
	Nameplates KING PELLINORE fitted w/e 30/1/60
	Isolating cock Steam brake pipes
22/11/62-22/12/62**LI**	108,223 Eastleigh
	326 monel metal stays riveted over 326 nuts renewed
	31 new small tubes 'Stewart and Lloyds'
22/3/65-30/4/65**HI**	Eastleigh 528 monel metal stays and 528 nuts renewed
	28 Foundation Ring rivets repaired
	2 fusible plugs

Boilers
No.1629 from new
No.1502 30/1/60
No.1002 22/12/62

Tenders
BR1F no.1297 from new
BR1C no.1013

Sheds
Nine Elms 19/12/55
Eastleigh 14/9/64
Nine Elms 27/6/66
Guildford 17/10/66

Withdrawn 3/67

73116

To traffic 15/11/55

Works
9/7/56	Not booked into works - ultrasonic axle test only at Eastleigh
21/2/57-14/3/57**NC**	44,399 Brighton
26/2/58-22/3/58**LI**	82,437 Eastleigh
	Briquette tube feeder modified
	Blowdown valve operating gear Diaphragm chains Isolating cock and gear
	T2263 Piston rod packing [Renewed and modified]
	T2299 Smokebox door chains
	460 monel metal stays riveted over 460 nuts renewed
	151 new small tubes 'Howell'
16/12/58-23/12/58**NC-LC**	104,336 Eastleigh
	T2263 and T2299 [both undisturbed]
6/4/59-11/4/59**NC**	123,704 Eastleigh
	T2263[U] and T2299 [U]
	4983 ATC equipment
2/9/59-19/9/59**NC-LC**	128,264 Eastleigh
	T2263 and T2299 [both undisturbed]
6/9/60-1/10/60**GO**	160,045 Eastleigh
	Injector overflow pipes Cab front window
2/8/62-13/11/62**LI-HI**	72,563 Eastleigh
	W/E 8/9/62 awaiting tender wheels
	W/E 15/9/62 nameplates ISEULT fitted
24/4/63-25/4/63**LC**	88,524 Eastleigh

Boilers
No.1624 from new
No.965 1/10/60

Tender
BR1F no.1298 from new

Sheds
Nine Elms 19/12/55
Bath Green Park 27/8/56
Eastleigh 27/10/56
Bath Green Park 19/7/57
Nine Elms 8/10/57
Bath Green Park 17/5/58
Nine Elms 13/10/58
Bath Green Park 13/6/59
Nine Elms 5/4/60
Eastleigh 14/9/64

Withdrawn 11/64

73116 ISEULT at Nine Elms, with just its cabside partly cleaned, to show number power classification and water treatment circle. Given the state the BR Class 5s soon fell in to after overhaul and the unlikelihood of them ever getting a regular clean, and the position, lack of prominence and style of the plates, it is hard to see why BR bothered. J.L. Stevenson, courtesy Hamish Stevenson.

73117

To traffic 25/11/55

Works
14/1/57-1/2/57**LC**	48,403 Brighton
	Washout plug holes in casing sides and back plates bushed and new washout plugs fitted
19/8/58-13/9/58**LI-HI**	113,398 Eastleigh
	Blowdown valve operating gear Isolating cock
	Smokebox chains Briquette container changed
	T2263 Piston rod packing [R]
	T2272 Piston heads [renewed 3 rings]
	40 copper stays riveted over
	151 new small tubes 'Stewart and Lloyds'
15/10/58-21/10/58**NCReturn**	114,823 Eastleigh T2263 T2272[U]
27/1/59-11/2/59**NC**	129,092 Eastleigh
	4983 ATC equipment
	T2263[U] T2272[U]
6/3/61-15/4/61**GO**	220,328 Eastleigh
	Draught screens
	T2291 Tender coalhole door plates modified for easier access
	W/E 8/4/61 heavy boiler repairs
	W/E 15/4/61 nameplates VIVIEN fitted
15/2/63**LC**	St.Lane Elec Depot
5/6/63-14/6/63**LC**	81,057 Eastleigh
17/2/64-28/3/64**LI-HI**	Eastleigh
22/12/64-15/1/65**LC**	Eastleigh
7/3/66-16/3/66**LC**	Eastleigh
20/4/66-22/4/66**NC**	Eastleigh

Boiler
No.1630 from new

Tender
BR1F no.1299 from new

Sheds
Nine Elms 19/12/55
Eastleigh 14/9/64
Nine Elms 27/6/66
Guildford 17/10/66

Withdrawn 3/67

Perhaps the filthiest one yet, VIVIEN, plates long gone, still attracts admirers at Dorchester South with the 8.35am Waterloo-Weymouth, 2 January 1967. J.L. Stevenson, courtesy Hamish Stevenson.

73117 VIVIEN at Feltham shed on 16 March 1963, top lamp going on at the front. VIVIEN had been another of those loaned to the Western when the Kings came a cropper. Four stud attachment of the return crank clearly visible. Stephen Gradidge.

73118

To traffic 12/55

Works
1/4/57-18/4/57**NC**   61,396 Brighton
Washout plugs holes bushed casing sides and back plate
14/1/58-8/2/58**LI-HI**   95,850 Eastleigh
Briquette tube feeder modified
H.O.9089 Cab pipes modified for access to plugs
Blowdown operating gear,
Smokebox door and diaphragm chains
T2263 piston rod packing [overhauled and modified]
30 new small tubes 'Howell'
12/11/59-20/11/59**NC**   184,231 Eastleigh
T2263 Piston rod packing [U]
T2299 Smokebox door stop chains [U]
4983ATC equipment
26/1/60-20/2/60**LI-HI**   192,077 Eastleigh
T2263 [R] T2299[examined]
Isolating cock Injector overflow pipes
Draught screens Cab windows
Nameplates KING LEODEGRANCE fitted W/E 20/2/60
370 monel metal stays riveted over 370 nuts renewed
12/12/62-2/2/63**GO**   296,421 Eastleigh
2 SR type fusible plugs
W/E 26/1/63 late boiler due to exceptional weather conditions
589 monel metal stays renewed 589 nuts renewed
151 new small tubes 'Stewart and Lloyds'

Boilers
No.1631 from new
No.853 2/2/63

Tender
BR1F no.1300 from new

Sheds
Nine Elms 19/12/55
Eastleigh 14/9/64
Nine Elms 27/6/66
Guildford 17/10/66

Withdrawn 9/7/67

73118 up train approaching Vauxhall in August 1965 - note short reach rod. Peter Groom.

73118 KING LEODEGRANCE at Nine Elms shed; short reach rod, lamp on 'stowing iron' in cab. Peter Groom.

73119

To traffic 9/12/55

Works
31/10/56-17/11/56**NC**	34,750 Brighton
6/2/58-22/2/58**LI**	96,831 Eastleigh
	Briquette tube feeder modified
	Blowdown valve operating gear
	Smokebox door and diaphragm chains,
	Cab pipes for access to washout plugs
	T2263 Piston rod packing [overhauled and modified]
	306 monel metal stays riveted over 306 nuts renewed
	30 new small tubes 'Howell'
25/5/59-11/6/59**NC**	161,199 Eastleigh
	T2263[U]
	T2299 [Smokebox door stop chains[U]
	Isolating cock
	4983ATC equipment
	Nameplates ELAINE fitted W/C 13/6/59
11/3/60-2/4/60**LI**	191,433 Eastleigh
	T2263 [R] T2299 [refitted]
	Tender lateral clearance to 3/SL/DE/20162,
	Injector overflow pipes
	151 new small tubes supplied by Swindon works
2/9/60-17/9/60**LC**	210,112 Eastleigh
1/2/62-10/3/62**GO**	26,577 Eastleigh
	W/E 3/3/62 awaiting boiler
	878 copper stays riveted over 878 nuts renewed 2 fusible plugs
15/11/62-22/11/62**LC**	22,871 Eastleigh
31/3/64-24/4/64**LC**	Eastleigh
26/4/66-6/5/66**LC**	Eastleigh 130 monel metal stays riveted over 130 nuts renewed

Boilers
No.1626 from new
No.840 10/3/62

Tender
BR1F No.1301 from new

Sheds
Nine Elms 19/12/55
Eastleigh 14/9/64

Withdrawn 3/67

73119, ELAINE that was, with a down train at Walton on the LWSR main line, 24 September 1966, viewed from 'Sir Richard's Bridge'. It was withdrawn in March the following year. The furthest, overgrown line, led to carriage sidings while the nearest line was part of the down goods yard. Stephen Gradidge.

73120

To traffic 12/55

Works
4/10/57-2/11/57**HI**	St.Rollox
16/2/59-17/3/59**LC[EO]**	Cowlairs
6/8/59-29/8/59**LI**	Cowlairs
13/10/59-31/10/59**LC[EO]**	Cowlairs
9/4/60-21/4/60**NC[EO]**	Cowlairs
26/4/60-14/5/60**NC[EO]**	Cowlairs
4/1/61-10/1/61**NC[EO]**	Cowlairs
29/5/61-14/7/61**GO**	Cowlairs
29/3/62-24/5/62**NC[EO]**	Cowlairs
24/1/63-1/3/63**HI**	Cowlairs
1/4/63-20/4/63**LC[EO]**	Cowlairs
14/5/65-5/6/65**LC**	Cowlairs
18/10/65-6/11/65**NC**	Cowlairs
16/4/66-12/5/66**LC[EO]**	Cowlairs

Tenders
No.1302 from new
No.1283

Sheds
Perth 10/1/56
Corkerhill 28/12/62

Withdrawn 31/12/66

Above. Back to Scotland for 73120, long a Perth engine and now for its last few years on the Corkerhill complement, at Stranraer on 31 July 1965. J.L. Stevenson, courtesy Hamish Stevenson.

Below. Perth's 73120, in excellent condition (it should be, it's only a couple of months old) at its home shed Perth, on 31 March 1956. It was one of a batch of five for the Scottish Region, the others going to Corkerhill. It being winter, no time had been wasted fitting a snowplough, the brackets and bolthole modifications being done during a visit to the substantial repair shop at Perth. J.L. Stevenson, courtesy Hamish Stevenson.

73121

To traffic 1/56

Works
3/2/58-1/3/58**LI**	Cowlairs
31/8/59-10/9/59**NC**	Cowlairs
14/3/60-30/4/60**GO**	Cowlairs
25/8/62-29/9/62**HI**	Cowlairs
3/1/63-12/1/63**NC[EO]**	Cowlairs
2/7/64-19/9/64**LI**	Cowlairs
22/4/65-29/5/65**LC**	Cowlairs
26/8/65-4/9/65**LC**	Cowlairs
24/11/65-27/11/65**NC**	Cowlairs

Tenders
BR1B no.1303 from new
BR1B no.1304 7/8/64
BR1B no.1288 26/6/65

Shed
Corkerhill 19/1/56

Withdrawn 1/2/66

73124 (tablet catcher fitting on cabside) passing Dalry with a Glasgow-Ayr relief (indicated by the 296 scrawled on the smokebox door) on 15 July 1957. The Caledonian-type semaphore route indicator is a real survival of an earlier age! 'BR5' on buffer beam. J.L. Stevenson, courtesy Hamish Stevenson.

73122

To traffic 1/56
Two Engine Record Cards at the National Archives with different details as shown below:-

Works		Works	
11/6/58-28/6/58**LI**	Cowlairs	9/6/58-28/6/58**LI**	Cowlairs
11/2/60-19/3/60**LI**	Cowlairs	27/1/60-19/3/60**LI**	Cowlairs
7/9/60-7/10/60**HC[EO]**	Cowlairs	30/8/60-17/10/60**HC[EO]**	Cowlairs
19/9/61**NC[EO]**	Cowlairs	13/9/61-19/9/61**NC[EO]**	Cowlairs
1/5/62**NC[EO]**	Cowlairs	25/4/62-1/5/62**NC[EO]**	Cowlairs
21/9/62-26/10/62**LI**	Cowlairs	12/9/62-26/10/62**LI**	Cowlairs
13/11/62-14/11/62**NC[EO]**	Cowlairs	6/11/62-14/11/62**NC[EO]**	Cowlairs
10/10/63-11/10/63**NC[EO]**	Cowlairs	27/9/63-11/10/63**NC[EO]**	Cowlairs
1/10/64-3/10/64**NC[EO]**	Cowlairs	10/9/64-3/10/64**NC[EO]**	Cowlairs
17/11/64-28/11/64 **LC**	Cowlairs	19/10/64-28/11/64**LC**	Cowlairs

Tenders
BR1B no.1304 from new
BR1 no.799 17/9/60
BR1B no.1304 15/10/61
BR1B no.1303 7/8/64

Shed
Corkerhill 30/1/56

Withdrawn 10/9/65

73123

To traffic 10/2/56

Works
12/5/58-6/6/58**LI**	Cowlairs
8/2/60-2/4/60**HI**	Cowlairs
14/11/61-6/1/62**GO**	Cowlairs
31/10/62-15/11/62**LC[EO]**	Cowlairs
23/7/64-7/8/64**NC[EO]**	Cowlairs
7/9/64-12/9/64**NC[EO]**	Cowlairs
8/2/65-27/2/65**LC**	Cowlairs

Tender
BR1B no.1305 from new

Shed
Corkerhill 18/2/56

Withdrawn 8/5/65

73124

To traffic 24/2/56

Works
25/3/58-19/4/58**LI**	Cowlairs
15/3/60-9/4/60**HI**	Cowlairs
3/6/60-10/6/60**NC[EO]**	Cowlairs
13/12/60-14/12/60**NC**	Cowlairs
16/1/62**NC[EO]**	Cowlairs
14/3/62-19/4/62**GO**	Cowlairs
31/10/62-10/11/62**L C**	Cowlairs
4/1/63-5/1/63**NC[EO]**	Cowlairs
7/5/63-17/5/63**LC[EO]**	Cowlairs
6/5/64-16/5/64**LC[EO]**	Cowlairs
2/10/64-8/10/64**CAS**	Cowlairs
26/11/64-27/11/64**NC**	Cowlairs
6/4/65-10/4/65**NC[EO]**	Cowlairs

Tender
BR1B no.1306 from new

Shed
Corkerhill 24/2/56

Withdrawn 6/12/65

73125

To traffic 6/7/56

Works
6/4/57-16/4/57	Swindon ATC equipment E4983
4/2/59-27/2/59**LC**	85,192 Derby
	R5900 Safety links between engine and tender
	R9129 Continuous blowdown gear
12/8/61-27/9/61**HI**	144,838 Derby
15/8/63-16/10/63**HC[CB]**	Crewe
8/6/65-14/8/65**HI**	Cowlairs

Annual mileage
1956 19,046
1957 36,785
1958 26,235
1959 26,911
1960 26,685
1961 15,009
1962 27,753
1963 15,821

Boiler
No.1750 from new

Tender
BR1B no.1413 from new

Sheds
Shrewsbury 14/7/56
Patricroft 6/9/58

Withdrawn 29/6/68

The first with the Caprotti gear, 73125 at an unknown date and obviously undergoing attention to the cylinder; the do not move red flag flutters in the breeze. WR lamp irons. R.J. Buckley, Initial Photographics.

73126

To traffic 13/7/56

Works
27/1/59-20/2/59**LC[EO]**   90,703 Derby
　　　　　　　　　　　　E4983 ATC equipment
　　　　　　　　　　　　R9129 Continuous blowdown gear
21/3/61-5/5/61**GO**　　　　140,714 Derby
30/11/64-8/2/65**LI**　　　　Eastleigh MR loco.
　　　　　　　　　　　　W/E 9/1/65 awaiting diagrams [Caprotti valve gear]
　　　　　　　　　　　　W/E 16/1/65 diagrams recieved, work proceeding
　　　　　　　　　　　　W/E 23/1/65 awaiting Hardy Spicer couplings
　　　　　　　　　　　　484 monel metal stays riveted over 484 nuts renewed
　　　　　　　　　　　　151 small tubes welded
　　　　　　　　　　　　2 fusible plugs 12 brick arch studs

Annual mileage
1956 18,267
1957 35,994
1958 34,853
1959 24,874
1960 23,301
1961 24,027
1962 27,817
1963 22,522

Boilers
No.1751 from new
No.999 5/5/61

Tender
BR1B no.1414 from new

Sheds
Shrewsbury 14/7/56
Patricroft 6/9/58

Withdrawn 20/4/68

73126 at Shrewsbury on 17 November 1956; it was the second of a batch of ten Caprottis which arrived at the shed between July and October that year. Had there been more of a future for steam, then Caprotti gear might have become much more commonplace. A disadvantage was its high initial cost; it was complicated and in the rough and tumble of everyday service the advantages were diminished. To function at its best it probably needed a better 'working environment' than Walschaerts gear. J. Robertson, www.transporttreasury.co.uk

73127

To traffic 9/8/56

Works
30/1/57-1/2/57**U**	Wolverhampton
27/4/59-7/5/59**LC**	92,467 Rugby
1/12/59-24/12/59**NC[EO]**	110,765 Derby
	E4983 ATC equipment
	R9129 Continuous blowdown gear
29/3/61-25/4/61**LI**	138,757 Derby
10/5/61-8/6/61**LC[EO]**	68 Derby
3/7/61-21/8/61**LC[EO]**	833 Derby
5/9/63-25/1/64**GO**	Crewe

Annual mileage
1956 14,669
1957 34,178
1958 32,949
1959 29,013
1960 26,123
1961 11,931
1962 27,835
1963 14,054

Boiler
No.1752 from new

Tender
BR1B no.1415 from new

Sheds
Shrewsbury 11/8/56
Patricroft 6/9/58

Withdrawn 4/11/67

73128

To traffic 28/8/56

Works
4/2/59-18/2/59**LC**	85,654 Derby
	E4983 ATC equipment
	E9129 Continuous blowdown gear
1/6/59-25/6/59**LC**	95,638 Derby
28/8/60-9/9/60**LI**	120,748 Derby
26/5/61-15/6/61**LC[EO]**	21,155 Derby
11/9/63-17/12/63**GO**	Crewe

Annual mileage
1956 13,116
1957 39,473
1958 31,781
1959 25,179
1960 21,066
1961 24,945
1962 19,244
1963 15,067

Boiler
No.1753 from new

Tender
BR1B no.1416 from new

Sheds
Shrewsbury 8/9/56
Patricroft 6/9/58
Rowsley 8/2/64
Patricroft 2/5/64

Withdrawn 11/5/68

73129

To traffic 31/8/56

Works
27/2/59-17/3/59**LC[EO]**	84,636 Rugby
14/12/59-6/1/60**NC[EO]**	105,776 Derby
14/9/61-14/10/61**GO**	Cowlairs
18/10/61-21/10/61**NC[EO]**	Cowlairs
1/5/65-18/5/65**LI**	Cowlairs

Annual mileage
1956 13,073
1957 35,814
1958 30,516
1959 26,373
1960 24,032
1961 18,032
1962 28,316
1963 22,203

Boilers
No.1754 from new
No.1775 14/10/61

Tender
BR1B no.1417 from new

Sheds
Shrewsbury 0/9/56
Patricroft 6/9/58

Withdrawn 2/12/67, engine preserved at the Midland Railway Centre

A woebegone 73128 at Manchester Victoria on what looks like banking duty – possibly in the last year of steam, 1968. A look at others of this Caprotti batch new at Derby will reveal WR lamp irons, for they were bound for Shrewsbury, by then a Western shed. From there they certainly got deep into WR territory, several making it to Plymouth and Paignton in the summer of 1958 but after that they were removed to Patricroft. That shed soon put 'proper' irons back on once it got its hands on them in 1958, as 73128 demonstrates. J. Davenport, Initial Photographics.

73129 new at Derby on 31 August 1956. The Caprotti arrangement of the BR Class 5s had really been arrived at with the last two Class 5s, 44686 and 44687, with two completely separate cam shafts, one for each cylinder. This allowed each cylinder's valve events to be individually 'tuned.' The early LMS Caprotti Class 5s by contrast had a single drive from the leading axle between the frames with a single cam shaft running transversely across the frames and serving both cam boxes. R.J. Buckley, Initial Photographics.

73130

To traffic 12/9/56

Works
27/2/59-16/3/59**LC[EO]**   84,709 Derby
                             E4983 ATC equipment
                             R9129 Continuous blowdown gear
1/2/60-18/2/60**NC[EO]**   115,285 Horwich
16/8/61-21/9/61**LI**   149,345 Derby
22/2/62-8/3/62**NC**   Derby
26/9/63-17/1/64**GO**   Darlington

Annual mileage
1956 10,431
1957 37,936
1958 31,298
1959 33,368
1960 26,217
1961 18,143
1962 21,851
1963 15,437

Boiler
No.1756 from new

Tender
BR1B no.1418 from new

Sheds
Shrewsbury 6/10/56
Patricroft 6/9/58

Withdrawn 21/1/67

73130 at Llandudno Junction shed, 26 August 1964; these North Wales jobs were to become just about the last passenger work for Patricroft's Caprottis. H.C. Casserley, courtesy R.M. Casserley.

73131

To traffic 24/9/56

Works
1/4/59-14/4/59**LC[EO]**   94,273 Rugby
　　Bogie and tender tyres
22/10/59-17/11/59**LI**   106,418 Derby
　　E4983 ATC equipment
　　R9129 Continuous blowdown gear
18/6/62-13/8/62**GO**   Derby

Annual mileage
1956 10,827
1957 40,598
1958 29,088
1959 29,105
1960 36,407
1961 25,245
1962 20,930
1963 23,431

Boiler
No.1755 from new

Tender
BR1B no.1419 from new

Sheds
Shrewsbury 6/10/56
Patricroft 6/9/58

Withdrawn 20/1/68

A grim 73131 at Patricroft shed in April 1966. Compare with its condition on page 10! Colin Stacey, Initial Photographics.

73132

To traffic 4/10/56

Works
22/4/59-14/5/59**LC**   91,957 Derby
                        R9129 Continuous blowdown gear
14/12/59-5/1/60**NC**   109,714 Derby
                        E4983 ATC equipment
19/4/61-9/6/61**GO**   143,369 Derby
26/8/64-9/10/64**HI**   Derby

Annual mileage
1956 8,932
1957 39,715
1958 32,399
1959 28,736
1960 26,274
1961 23,567
1962 28,673
1963 22,332

Boilers
No.1757 from new
No.1186 9/6/61

Tender
BR1B no.1420 from new

Sheds
Shrewsbury 6/10/56
Patricroft 6/9/58

Withdrawn 30/3/68

73132 delivered to the shed yard at Derby on 6 October 1956. It has been said that Caprotti valve gear and superheating were the only two true advances after the establishment of the Stephensonian model of the steam locomotive. R.J. Buckley, Initial Photographics.

73132 at Manchester Exchange after arrival with the 11.55pm from Glasgow, on 22 July 1967; by now all the remaining Caprotti Class 5s were concentrated at Patricroft which thus operated the engines for a decade. The shed did not involve itself in the more complex repairs (which was only in keeping with its 'garage' status, after all) and did not hold a full range of spares. Replacements for damaged cams and so on would come from Crewe courtesy of a couple of fitters on overtime. Derby also had experts who were always being called out and presumably the same was true in Scotland where a bloke from the works would attend any trouble at St Rollox, say. The canny Scots kept the 'funnies' closer to home as it were. J.L. Stevenson, courtesy Hamish Stevenson.

73133

To traffic 11/10/56

Works
17/1/58-2/2/58**NC** Wolverhampton works
25/6/59-3/8/59**LC** 85,822 Derby
2/12/59-1/2/60**NC[EO]** 97,500 Derby
E4983 ATC equipment
R9129 Continuous blowdown gear
16/11/61-18/1/62**GO** Derby
30/6/64-12/8/64**LC** Darlington
15/9/65-27/10/65**HI** Eastleigh 52 copper stays riveted over 554 nuts renewed
151 new small tubes 'Stewart and Lloyds'
MR loco.

Annual mileage
1956 6,841
1957 37,835
1958 23,677
1959 29,147
1960 24,790
1961 15,130
1962 28,597
1963 24,679

Boilers
No.1758 from new
No.1187 18/1/62

Tender
BR1B no.1421 from new

Sheds
Shrewsbury 3/11/56
Patricroft 6/9/58

Withdrawn 29/6/68

73133 at its Shrewsbury home; WR ATC brake valve prominent by the side of the smokebox. This is the old LMS side and true to form, it contains largely the locos on former LM diagrams, the new Caprottis being in many senses 'LM' locomotives. It worked this way, presumably, because the LM fitters, their spares and tools, even the engine boards remained over this side; likewise the WR men and their equipment stayed over on 'their' side. The Shrewsbury Caprottis were 'Western', after all, for less than two years. A. Battson, www.transporttreasury.co.uk

Another tired Caprotti, at Patricroft in April 1965. 73133 has the hideous daubing which came to be something of a trademark.

73134

To traffic 18/10/56

Works
9/7/59-10/8/59**LC**	82,669 Derby
13/1/60-1/2/60**NC[EO]**	93,365 Derby
26/10/61-18/11/61**GO**	Cowlairs
28/5/65-8/7/65?	Cowlairs

Annual mileage
1956 6,631
1957 33,922
1958 26,284
1959 25,604
1960 27,721
1961 19,951
1962 22,986
1963 25,847

Boilers
No.1759 from new
No.1754 18/11/61

Tender
BR1B no.1422 from new

Sheds
Shrewsbury 3/11/56
Patricroft 6/9/58

Withdrawn 22/6/68

73135

To traffic 26/10/56

Works
12/2/57-20/2/57**NC[EO]**	11,086 Derby
9/1/59-3/2/59**LC[EO]**	89,998 Rugby Tyres
7/7/60-26/8/60**LI**	140,570 Derby
5/9/63-21/11/63**GO**	Crewe
4/12/63-7/12/63**NC[Rect]**	Crewe
25/6/64-22/8/64**LC**	Darlington

Annual mileage
1956 7,765
1957 43,852
1958 38,313
1959 35,731
1960 28,432

Boiler
No.1760 from new

Tender
BR1C no.1423 from new

Sheds
Holyhead 26/10/56
Leicester Midland 20/4/58
Derby 5/1/59
Rowsley 21/11/59
Derby 2/5/64
Patricroft 6/9/64

Withdrawn 30/3/68

Patricroft's Caprotti 73134 (AWS, shed on buffer beam) heading 45105 finds itself in an unexpected corner of BR on 17 July 1965. This is Stranraer Harbour and the Class 5s are in charge of 1N33, a train for Newcastle. On the left is the station pilot, a diesel shunter, and 44798 with a relief for St Enoch. J.L. Stevenson, courtesy Hamish Stevenson.

In a dishevelled state but doubtless running well, 73135 has found its way to Cricklewood (you'd expect the Rowsley ones to turn up but not Patricroft ones particularly) on 25 June 1960; smokebox in fearful state and chemical deposits from water leaking from the regulator rod gland. The pipe leading up to the dome takes steam from the regulator, as soon as it is opened, to seat the Caprotti inlet valves. Peter Groom.

Rowsley's 73135 in the wars at Derby works in the early 1960s. The only explanation for the damage is that something very heavy, a crane perhaps, fell on the roof. It must have been extremely alarming for the crew!

73136

To traffic 31/10/56

Works
14/5/57-22/5/57**NC[EO]**	22,624 Derby
29/4/59-27/5/59**LI**	Derby
6/12/60-4/1/61**LC[EO]**	51,409 Derby
6/11/61-7/12/61**LC**	Derby
13/11/62-14/12/62**GO**	Derby

Annual mileage
1956 7,070
1957 44,666
1958 43,928
1959 39,266
1960 26,045

Boiler
No.1761 from new

Tender
BR1C no.1424 from new

Sheds
Holyhead 31/10/56
Leicester Midland 20/4/58
Derby 5/1/59
Rowsley 21/11/59
Derby 2/5/64
Patricroft 14/6/64

Withdrawn 16/3/68

73137

To traffic 9/11/56

Works
30/12/58-30/1/59**LC[EO]**	94,112 Rugby
2/11/59-26/11/59**LI**	115,494 Derby
27/9/61-24/10/61**LC**	66,669 Derby
6/7/62-12/9/62**GO**	Derby
7/2/64-15/5/64**LC**	Darlington

Annual mileage
1956 6,026
1957 43,511
1958 44,575
1959 26,832
1960 40,842

Boiler
No.1762 from new

Tender
BR1C no.1425 from new

Sheds
Holyhead 9/11/56
Leicester Midland 20/4/58
Derby 14/6/58
Leicester Midland 12/7/58
Derby 10/1/59
Rowsley 21/11/59
Leicester Midland 19/5/62
Rowsley 18/6/62
Derby 2/5/64
Patricroft 14/6/64

Withdrawn 14/6/67

Rowsley Caprotti 73137 at Darlington shed, 19 April 1964. If the Caprotti gear failed at a place like this there would obviously be nil prospect of any remedial attention. Mind you, that was true of Leicester and any number of other sheds much closer to home! It will have been noted by now that the steam feed piping on the smokebox right-hand side has changed. With the Caprottis there was no need to feed atomiser steam for the mechanical lubricator, both the one below and the one on the other side. These were now both on the same right-hand side by the firebox and fed separately. The whistle had also moved so it was necessary now only to feed the tube steam cleaning lance valve on the smokebox rim. The position of the valve above, taking steam from the header, has moved forward, for convenience. Peter Groom.

Perhaps the worst front numberplate, on Caprotti 73137 at Patricroft shed on 18 February 1967. Otherwise the livery is the dreaded 'BR grey'; lamp irons re-arranged at the front but to an entirely aberrant pattern. The top one was supposed to move to the smokebox door; *an* iron certainly has but the top one remains in place. Of the re-arranged 'middle' iron on the buffer beam – no sign! I. Laidlaw, www.transporttreasury.co.uk

73138

To traffic 15/11/56

Works
6/5/57-31/5/57 **LC[EO]** 20,928 Derby Timken bearings
20/1/59-12/3/59 **LC[EO]** 96,036 Rugby
1/6/59-25/6/59 **LC** 103,098 Derby
17/11/60-18/12/60 **LI** 154,298 Derby MDL/1468
27/6/62-3/8/62 **HC** Derby
20/11/63-5/3/64 **GO** Darlington

Annual mileage
1956 3,310
1957 43,284
1958 43,364
1959 32,519
1960 32,686

Boiler
No.1763 from new

Tenders
BR1C no.1426 from new
BR1C no.1429 25/6/62

Sheds
Holyhead 15/11/56
Leicester Midland 27/1/57
Derby 10/1/59
Rowsley 21/11/59
Patricroft 14/6/64

Withdrawn 27/4/68

73139

To traffic 22/11/56

Works
20/1/59-11/2/59 **LC[EO]** 96,280 Derby
23/5/60-23/6/60 **HI** 152,124 Derby
22/10/62-16/11/62 **GO** Derby

Annual mileage
1956 5,002
1957 46,632
1958 41,675
1959 43,259
1960 35,853

Boiler
No.1764 from new

Tender
BR1C no.1427 from new

Sheds
Holyhead 22/11/56
Leicester Midland 26/4/58
Derby 10/1/59
Rowsley 21/11/59
Patricroft 14/6/64

Withdrawn 13/5/67

Or it might be this one, on 73139 awaiting departure from Birkenhead Woodside with a Paddington train would you believe, in March 1967. Terrible leakage through the gland where that regulator rodding mechanism is, spilling down over the running plate. There is some seriously awry piping in front of the driver's window.

73140

To traffic 29/11/56

Works
13/4/59-5/5/59**LI**	97,025 Derby
14/11/60-2/12/60**LC**	59,177 Derby
27/3/62-2/5/62**GO**	Derby

Annual mileage
1956 3,369
1957 42,348
1958 41,057
1959 35,838
1960 34,616

Boilers
No.1765 from new
No.1758 2/5/62

Tender
BR1C no.1428 from new

Sheds
Leicester Midland 1/12/56
Holyhead 27/1/57
Leicester Midland 20/4/58
Trafford Park 24/9/58
Derby 10/1/59
Rowsley 16/11/59
Derby 16/9/61
Rowsley 27/2/62
Patricroft 6/6/64

Withdrawn 10/67

73141

To traffic 6/12/56

Works
24/2/59-19/3/59**LC**	99,855 Derby
	Tyres
16/5/60-14/6/60**HI**	139,311 Derby
13/11/62-21/12/62**GO**	Derby
12/7/65-9/10/65**LC**	Cowlairs

Annual mileage
1956 2,405
1957 49,614
1958 41,857
1959 36,120
1960 33,905

Boiler
No.1766 from new

Tenders
BR1C no.1429 from new
BR1C no.1426 25/6/62 at Rowsley shed

Sheds
Leicester Midland 6/12/56
Derby 10/1/59
Rowsley 16/11/59
Patricroft 14/6/64

Withdrawn 29/7/67

A wholly filthy (so filthy that the said filth actually has *texture*, which is only acquired by depth) 73141 of Derby heads a train at Mill Hill on 16 August 1959. It was only the Midland line Caprottis that ventured to London with any regularity. Stephen Gradidge.

73142

To traffic 13/12/56

Works
18/2/59-16/3/59**LI**	91,991 Derby
	MDL/1414 Shot peened laminated springs on coupled wheels
16/11/61-20/12/61**HI**	Derby
23/12/63-29/2/64**GO**	Darlington
12/3/64-6/5/64	[Information incomplete on ERC]

Annual mileage
1956 91
1957 49,531
1958 38,586
1959 40,901
1960 35,650

Boiler
No.1767 from new

Tender
BR1C No.1430 from new

Sheds
Leicester Midland 18/12/56
Derby 5/1/59
Rowsley 16/11/59
Derby 2/5/64
Patricroft 14/6/64

Withdrawn 27/4/68

Heroic 73142 at Kingmoor on 10 August 1965; despite its atrocious condition it had nearly three more years of work ahead of it. Peter Groom.

73143

To traffic 20/12/56

Works
11/6/59-22/6/59**LC**	100,148 Derby Tyres
5/7/60-15/8/60**HI**	137,005 Derby
27/8/63-25/10/63**GO**	Crewe
18/2/65-20/2/65**NC[EO]**	Cowlairs

Annual mileage
1956 134
1957 41,130
1958 44,519
1959 32,209
1960 34,542

Boiler
No.1768 from new

Tender
No.1431 from new

Sheds
Leicester Midland 20/12/56
Nottingham 14/4/58
Derby 14/1/59
Rowsley 16/11/59
Patricroft 23/2/64

Withdrawn 29/6/68

73144

To traffic 28/12/56

Works
13/5/59-21/5/59**LC**	109,592 Derby Tyres
8/8/60-8/9/60**HI**	159,156 Derby
21/5/62-8/6/62**LI**	Derby
4/12/63-1/4/64**GO**	Darlington
16/2/66-9/4/66**LC**	Cowlairs
20/4/66-23/4/66**LC[EO]**	Cowlairs

Annual mileage
1956 30
1957 46,894
1958 47,804
1959 43,004
1960 33,867

Boiler
No.1769 from new

Tender
BR1C No.1432 from new

Sheds
Leicester Midland 28/12/56
Nottingham 14/4/58
Derby 4/2/59
Rowsley 16/11/59
Derby 26/9/61
Rowsley 10/2/62
Derby 2/5/64
Patricroft 14/6/64

Withdrawn 26/8/67

Patricroft's 73143 climbing Shap, banked in the rear, in August 1964. J.G. Walmsley, www.transporttreasury.co.uk

Perhaps the worst condition a locomotive can descend to, short of the scrap line. This is 73143 inside its Patricroft home on 3 June 1968; it was withdrawn within days and may well have not worked for a while. Its official demise came in the two week period ended 29 June 1968; Patricroft closed on 1 July and it was at last *finis* for the British Caprotti valve gear – it did well to last more or less to The End. C. Stacey, Initial Photographics.

In its happier Midland line times, 73143 (then of Nottingham) pilots 44828 on the up Palatine leaving Derby station, 2 April 1958. R.J. Buckley, Initial Photographics.

73145

To traffic 24/1/57

Works
5/11/58-22/11/58**LI**	Cowlairs
22/6/59-1/7/59**LC[EO]**	St.Rollox
13/9/60-23/9/60**LC[EO]**	Cowlairs
22/2/61-29/4/61**GO**	Cowlairs
18/3/63-20/4/63**LC**	Cowlairs
29/1/64-7/3/64**HI**	Cowlairs
15/12/65-18/12/65**NC[EO]**	Cowlairs
30/5/66-17/6/66**LC**	Cowlairs

Boiler
No.1770 from new

Tender
BR1B no.1433 from new

Sheds
St.Rollox 26/1/57
Eastfield 26/12/65
Ayr 24/9/66

Withdrawn 26/9/66

A gleaming 73145 new at Derby shed on 26 January 1957. After running in by Derby shed (the running foremen there were the luckiest around, you'd have to think) each new Class 5 would be despatched on the next available job if not direct to its intended home but certainly in the general direction thereof. R.J. Buckley, Initial Photographics.

73146

To traffic 12/1/57

Works
12/11/58-6/12/58**LI**	Cowlairs
8/6/59-5/8/59**LC[EO]**	Cowlairs
29/11/60-7/1/61**LI**	Cowlairs
2/11/61-11/11/61**NC[EO]**	Cowlairs
17/12/62-2/2/63**GO**	Cowlairs
20/1/64-6/2/64**LC[EO]**	Cowlairs
31/12/64-30/1/65**HI**	Cowlairs
2/6/65-10/7/65**LC**	Cowlairs
10/8/65-4/9/65**NC**	Cowlairs
29/11/65-11/12/65**NC[EO]**	Cowlairs
19/1/66-12/2/66**LC**	Cowlairs

Boiler
No.1771 from new

Tender
BR1B no.1434 from new

Sheds
St.Rollox 23/1/57
Eastfield 26/12/65
Motherwell 10/11/66

Withdrawn 1/5/67

Eastfield's 73146 on a Glasgow-Aberdeen football train, passing St Rollox shed on 20 February 1965. It is being assisted in the rear by NBL Type 2 D6135. J.L. Stevenson, courtesy Hamish Stevenson.

73147

To traffic 13/2/57

Works
8/12/58-27/12/58**LI**	Cowlairs
30/6/59-8/7/59**NC[EO]**	St.Rollox
24/11/59-11/12/59**NC[EO]**	Cowlairs
10/10/60-19/10/60**LC[EO]**	Cowlairs
11/1/62-13/1/62**LC[EO]**	Cowlairs
1/8/62-11/8/62**LC[EO]**	Cowlairs
5/11/64-5/12/64**LC**	Cowlairs

Boiler
No.1772 from new

Tender
BR1B no.1435 from new

Shed
St.Rollox 23/2/57

Withdrawn 21/8/65

73148

To traffic 7/3/57

Works
12/12/58-31/12/58**LI**	Cowlairs
11/6/59-12/6/59**NC[EO]**	St.Rollox
28/6/60-8/7/60**LC[EO]**	Cowlairs
11/5/61-20/5/61**GO**	Cowlairs
30/11/62-5/12/62**LC[EO]**	Cowlairs
23/12/63-25/1/64**HI**	Cowlairs
20/5/64**NC[EO]**	Cowlairs
29/3/65-3/4/65**LC**	Cowlairs

Boiler
No.1773 from new

Tender
BR1B no.1436 from new

Shed
St.Rollox 16/3/57

Withdrawn 20/9/65

73147 at St Rollox shed on 4 August 1957. Proximity to works was a good thing for these unconventional locos, and specialist fitters could be summoned at short notice. A.G. Forsyth, Initial Photographics.

73148 ready for despatch to Scotland, 9 March 1957. R.J. Buckley, Initial Photographics.

73148 at Perth on 23 March 1957. As this sequence shows it contrived to look relatively respectable through most of its working life, or at least James Stevenson caught it on a good day/days! Simple '5' above running number. On the running plate, next to the rear sand cover is a lever mechanism, rather like a large dip-stick. This operated the blow down valve at the bottom of the firebox. It was not confined to the Caprottis and not all engines had it, by any means. J.L. Stevenson, courtesy Hamish Stevenson.

At Perth again, with the 4.0pm Dundee-Glasgow, 1 July 1961; at first 73148 looks fairly respectable, with the number and shedplate picked out nicely in that Scottish style, and B.R.5 on the buffer beam. Letting the side down a bit, however, it is running without a dome cover... J.L. Stevenson, courtesy Hamish Stevenson.

Finally at Glasgow Buchanan Street on the 3.15pm for Dundee, 29 February 1964. Our 'dipstick' visible again. J.L. Stevenson, courtesy Hamish Stevenson.

73149

To traffic 20/3/57

Works
16/9/57-26/9/57 **LC** St.Rollox
18/12/58-10/1/59 **LI** Cowlairs
8/6/59-11/6/59 **NC[EO]** St.Rollox
1/8/60-26/8/60 **LC[EO]** Cowlairs
26/12/61-27/1/62 **GO** Cowlairs
24/3/65-10/4/65 **LI** Cowlairs

Boiler
No.1774 from new

Tenders
BR1B no.1437 from new
BR1B no.1438

Sheds
St.Rollox 13/4/57
Stirling 26/11/66

Withdrawn 9/12/66

Blasting departure from Aberdeen for 73149 with the Granite City for Glasgow, 28 August 1965. Paul Cotterell.

73150

To traffic 4/4/57

Works
22/12/58-16/1/59**LI**	Cowlairs
24/10/59-11/12/59**LC[EO]**	Cowlairs
8/5/61-17/6/61**GO**	Cowlairs
11/2/63-21/2/63**NC[EO]**	Cowlairs
19/3/64-25/4/64**HI**	Cowlairs

Boiler
No.1775 from new

Tenders
BR1B no.1438 from new
BR1B no.1437 no date

Sheds
St.Rollox 13/4/57
Stirling 26/11/66

Withdrawn 9/12/66

73151

To traffic 18/4/57

Works
20/1/59-13/2/59**LI**	Cowlairs
1/9/60-16/9/60**LC**	Cowlairs
2/6/61-12/8/61**GO**	Cowlairs
5/2/62-22/2/62**LC[EO]**	Cowlairs
11/11/64-26/12/64**HI**	Cowlairs
4/2/65-6/2/65**NC**	Cowlairs
7/5/65-17/5/65**LC**	Cowlairs

Boiler
No.1776 from new

Tenders
BR1B no.1439 from new
BR1B no.1440 17/11/64

Shed
St.Rollox 11/5/57

Withdrawn 22/8/66

73150 looking exquisite at Derby on 6 April 1957. Injector steam valves show very clearly in front of the cab, with operating pipes running back horizontally into the cab. The St Rollox batch largely stayed at their home shed, which was as it should be though near the end one or two were sent to see out their days at sheds like Ayr, Motherwell and Stirling where the foreman fitters would have scratched their heads a bit. R.J. Buckley, Initial Photographics.

73151 with noticeably larger cab numbers ('5MT' above) at St Rollox, 20 February 1965; 73147 behind. J.L. Stevenson, courtesy Hamish Stevenson.

73152

To traffic 9/5/57
Two Engine History Cards (ERCs) at the National Archive
Works

13/2/59-28/2/59**LI**	Cowlairs	19/2/59-28/2/59**LI**	Cowlairs
17/4/59-20/4/59**NC[EO]**	Cowlairs	13/4/59-20/4/59**NC[EO]**	Cowlairs
1/3/61-8/4/61**GO**	Cowlairs	6/2/61-7/4/61**GO**	Cowlairs
12/12/61-15/12/61**LC[EO]**	Cowlairs	27/11/61-15/12/61**LC[EO]**	Cowlairs
14/12/62-21/12/62**LC**	Cowlairs	10/12/62-21/12/62**LC**	Cowlairs
18/11/63-7/12/63**LI**	Cowlairs	30/10/63-7/12/63**LI**	Cowlairs
13/12/63-17/12/63**NC[EO]**	Cowlairs	13/12/63-17/12/63**NC[EO]**	Cowlairs
13/5/64-15/5/64**NC[EO]**	Cowlairs	28/4/64-15/5/64**NC[EO]**	Cowlairs
4/6/64-12/6/64**NC[EO]**	Cowlairs	22/5/64-12/6/64**NC[EO]**	Cowlairs
16/10/64**NC[EO]***	Cowlairs	16/10/64**LC**	Cowlairs
12/5/65-22/5/65**LC**	Cowlairs	12/5/65-22/5/65**LC**	Cowlairs

*****LC** crossed out

Boiler
No.1777 from new

Tenders
BR1B no.1440 from new
BR1B no.1439 17/11/64

Shed
St.Rollox 11/4/57

Withdrawn 6/12/65

73153

To traffic 24/5/57

Works
4/2/59-27/2/59**LI**	Cowlairs
4/7/60-15/7/60**LC[EO]**	Cowlairs
11/1/61-18/2/61**GO**	Cowlairs
27/11/61-20/12/61**LC[EO]**	Cowlairs
8/11/62-1/12/62**LI**	Cowlairs
4/6/63-15/6/63**LC[EO]**	Cowlairs
25/3/64-1/5/64**LC[EO]**	Cowlairs
13/5/64-20/5/64**NC[EO]**	Cowlairs
25/6/64-15/7/64**LC[EO]**	Cowlairs
14/12/64-26/12/64**LC[EO]**	Cowlairs
11/1/65-16/2/65**NC[EO]**	Cowlairs
3/2/66-5/3/66**LC[EO]**	Cowlairs

Boiler
No.1778 from new

Tender
BR1B no.1441 from new

Sheds
St.Rollox 8/6/57
Stirling 26/11/66

Withdrawn 9/12/66

73154

To traffic 14/6/57

Works
6/3/59-28/3/59**LI**	Cowlairs
4/11/60-25/11/60**LC[EO]**	Cowlairs
23/1/62-24/2/62**GO**	Cowlairs
13/2/63-6/4/63**LC[EO]**	Cowlairs
26/12/63-18/1/64**LC[EO]**	Cowlairs
19/6/64**LC[EO]**	Cowlairs
3/5/65-12/5/65**LI**	Cowlairs

Boiler
No.1779 from new

Tender
BR1B no.1442 from new

Sheds
St.Rollox 6/7/57
Stirling 21/12/65
Motherwell 13/6/66

Withdrawn 31/12/66

73154, the last of the St Rollox ten, ready at Derby on 13 June 1957. R.J. Buckley, Initial Photographics.

73155

To traffic 19/12/56

Works
7/1/64-25/1/64**NC-LC**   68,723 Eastleigh
                           4983 ATC equipment
                           Overflow pipes and clips
17/8/65-1/9/65   550 monel metal stays riveted over 550 nuts renewed
                           2 fusible plugs
4/4/66   60 monel metal stays riveted over 60 nuts renewed

Boilers
No.1780 from new
No.1190 25/1/61

Tender
BR1B no.1443 from new

Sheds
Neasden 19/1/57
Millhouses 20/4/58
Canklow 31/12/61
Eastleigh 17/12/62
Feltham 6/1/64
Eastleigh 20/11/64
Guildford 25/3/67

Withdrawn 9/7/67

73156

To traffic 19/12/56

Works
3/2/59-19/3/59**HI**   96,692 Doncaster
14/11/59-1/12/59**LC**   125,401 Doncaster
31/10/61-15/12/61**GO**   Derby
31/1/63-2/2/63**HC**   Derby
                             E4983 ATC equipment
27/5/65-8/6/65**HC**   Cowlairs

Annual mileage
1960 39,297

Boilers
No.1781 from new
No.1498 15/12/61
No.1498 8/6/65

Tender
BR1B no.1444 from new

Sheds
Neasden 22/12/56
Millhouses 20/4/58
Grimesthorpe 4/1/59
Derby 11/9/60
Neasden 22/9/60
Leicester Central 30/6/62
Woodford Halse 24/2/63
Cricklewood 12/5/63
Leamington Spa 5/10/64
Tyseley 22/5/65
Bolton 30/4/66

Withdrawn 6/67, engine preserved

73156, AWS battery box below the cab, at Woodford Halse shed on 12 April 1963. It has had a cloth wiped over it lately and even the yellow on the Timken tender axleboxes is showing through. It was one of a batch of five (deliveries were nearly always in multiples of five) that had gone new to Neasden. None stayed long, although four out of the five came back at least once after spells at all manner of sheds on the LMR, which had taken over the GC. Stephen Gradidge.

73157

To traffic 28/12/56

Works
16/2/59-23/3/59**LI**	88,331 Derby
18/9/60-24/11/60**LC[EO]**	64,299 Derby
24/3/61-11/5/61**LI**	83,211 Derby
18/11/64-8/1/65**LI-HI**	Eastleigh
	MR loco.
	W/E 26/12/64 repairs nearly complete
	W/E 2/1/65 on test
	Studs and seams caulked rivets renewed 2 fusible plugs

Annual mileage
1956 74
1957 63,703
1958 18,225
1959 40,309
1960 32,771

Boilers
No.1782 from new
No.1762 8/1/65

Tender
BR1B no.1445 from new

Sheds
Neasden 19/1/57
Kings Cross 20/10/57
Darnall 19/10/58
Neasden 14/12/58
Derby 21/2/59
Neasden 18/6/60
Cricklewood 30/6/62
Chester Midland 22/5/63
Woodford Halse 2/11/63
Oxley 16/1/65
Patricroft 3/4/65

Withdrawn 11/5/68

73158

To traffic 28/12/56

Works
28/10/58-17/11/58**HC**   84,529 Doncaster
18/5/59-4/6/59**LC**   Derby Tyres
10/5/60-17/6/60**LI**   135,931 Derby
6/10/61-21/11/61**LC[EO]**   68,364 Derby
30/4/62-1/6/62**GO**   Derby
19/3/65-27/3/65**LC**   Cowlairs

Annual mileage
1957 62,078
1958 23,306
1959 35,999
1960 49,825

Boilers
No.1783 from new
No.1781

Tender
BR1B no.1446 from new

Sheds
Neasden 28/12/56
Kings Cross 20/10/57
Darnall 19/10/58
Neasden 28/12/58
Derby 12/2/59
Neasden 13/6/60
Cricklewood 30/6/62
Bedford 24/6/63
Cricklewood 29/7/63
Patricroft 19/4/64

Withdrawn 14/10/67

73158 on the 8.25am Manchester-Scarborough, leaving Huddersfield on 22 July 1967; long-term leak from one of the rivets securing the baffles inside the tender tank. J.L. Stevenson, courtesy Hamish Stevenson.

73159

To traffic 11/1/57

Works
6/2/59-27/2/59**LI**	Derby
	M/D/L 1414 Shot peened laminated springs on coupled wheels
7/10/59-5/11/59**LC[EO]**	30,102 Derby
5/12/60-31/12/60**LC[EO]**	77,987 Nottingham
25/9/61-30/10/61**LI**	106,087 Derby
9/8/62-31/8/62**HC**	Derby
1/5/63-10/5/63**NC**	Derby
8/3/63-24/4/63**HC**	Derby
	Boiler
1/5/63-10/5/63**NC**	Derby
30/9/63-12/10/63**LC**	Bolton
15/4/64**CAS**	Darlington
14/9/64-26/10/64**LI**	Eastleigh
	435 monel metal stays riveted over 435 nuts renewed
	Rivets studs and seams caulked 2 fusible plugs. MR loco.

Annual mileage
1957 52,826
1958 32,867
1959 36,309
1960 44,459

Boilers
No.1784 from new
No.1766 26/10/64

Tender
BR1B no.1447 from new

Sheds
Neasden 11/1/57
Kings Cross 20/10/57
Darnall 15/11/58
Neasden 28/12/58
Derby 12/2/59
Neasden 13/6/60
Leicester Central 30/6/62
Woodford Halse 12/1/63
Nuneaton 19/9/64
Patricroft 18/7/65

Withdrawn 28/10/67

73160

To traffic 23/1/57

Works
2/9/59-14/10//59**HI**	Doncaster E/DN/L/68 Clearance on firebox support brackets
3/7/64-28/8/64**LI**	Eastleigh MR loco.
	430 monel metal stays riveted over 430 nuts renewed
	151 new small tubes 'Stewart and Lloyds'
	Internal boiler exam on frames
	Rivets and seams caulked 2 fusible plugs
19/1/65-9/2/65**LC**	Eastleigh MR loco.

Boiler
No.1785 from new

Tender
BR1B no.1448 from new

Sheds
Blaydon 1/2/57
Gateshead 10/2/57
Normanton 15/9/57
Bletchley 19/4/64
Oxley 16/1/65
Patricroft 28/6/65

Withdrawn 11/11/67

73161

To traffic 27/1/57

Works
27/5/59-2/7/59HI
30/7/62-24/8/62LI
3/7/63-2/8/63**Cas**
17/1/64-15/2/64**LC**

Darlington
Crewe
Horwich
Eastleigh. WR loco.

Boiler
No.1786 27/1/57

Tender
BR1B no.1449 from new

Sheds
Blaydon 1/2/57
Gateshead 10/2/57
Normanton 15/9/57
Neville Hill 17/6/62
Wakefield 16/6/63
Exmouth Jct. 28/9/63

Withdrawn 12/64

73161, AWS fitted, during its days as a Normanton engine and quite possibly at that very shed, about 1961 perhaps. Paul Chancellor Collection.

73162

To traffic 15/2/57

Works
22/4/59-23/5/59HI   Doncaster

Boiler
No.1787 from new

Tender
BR1B no.1450 from new

Sheds
York 16/2/57
Huddersfield 2/11/58
Neville Hill 17/6/61
Wakefield 16/6/63
Exmouth Jct. 28/9/63
Oxford 10/1/65

Withdrawn 5/65

73163

To traffic 2/57
No Engine Record Card at National Archives
Engine Record card at NRM shows no Works visits

Boiler
No.1788 from new

Tender
BR1B no.1451 from new

Sheds
York 16/3/57
Huddersfield 15/11/58
Wakefield 12/9/64
Oxley 7/11/64
Patricroft 3/4/65

Withdrawn 20/11/65

73162 approaching Saxelby tunnel, between Melton Mowbray and Nottingham, with a down evening express, 28 August 1959. A North Eastern Region engine from new it was in a run of ten allocated to York at first. It was never allocated to the LM but managed spells on both the Southern and the Western in the last year of its life. Peter Groom.

The Book of the BR Standard Class 5 4-6-0s

73164

To traffic 5/3/57

Works
29/5/57-3/6/57**Adj**	Doncaster
15/6/59-28/7/59**HI**	Doncaster
22/11/62-28/12/62**HC**	Derby

Boiler
No.1789 from new

Tender
BR1B no.1452 from new

Sheds
York 16/3/57
Huddersfield 2/11/58
Bath Green Park 28/9/63
Bristol Barrow Road 30/11/63
Oxford 12/10/64

Withdrawn 12/64

73165

To traffic 3/57
No Engine Record Card
at National Archive
Engine Record Card at NRM
lists no works visits

Works
12/1/65-?**LI**	Eastleigh MR loco

Boilers
No.1790 from new
No.1453 26/2/65

Tender
BR1B no.1453 from new

Sheds
York 16/3/57
Huddersfield 15/11/58
Wakefield 12/9/64
Oxley 7/11/64
Patricroft 3/4/65

Withdrawn 2/10/65

73166 at Agecroft shed, resting over on a job from its home city, York, on 21 August 1958. The steam pipes to the clack this side is visible in its entirety. Peter Groom.

73166

To traffic 29/3/57

Works
30/7/59-5/9/59**HI** Doncaster
23/7/63 Crewe

Annual mileage
1959 39,129
1960 40,979
1961 22,415
1962 20,830

Boiler
No.1791 from new

Tender
BR1B no.1454 from new

Sheds
York 20/4/57
Huddersfield 2/11/58
Leeds Holbeck 19/4/59
Huddersfield 11/9/60
Leeds Holbeck 8/4/62
Royston 9/9/62
Patricroft 16/6/63
Exmouth Jct. 2/11/63
Yeovil Town 12/10/64
Oxford 11/7/65

Withdrawn 31/12/65

73167

To traffic 13/4/57

Works
4/57 E/DN/L/76 UK cast iron piston
20/9/57-30/9/57**NC** Doncaster
13/4/59-15/5/59**HI** Doncaster
4983 ATC equipment
14/8/62-5/9/62**HI** Derby
7/1/64-25/1/64**LC** 177,811 Eastleigh
Overflow pipes and clips
17/9/64-14/10/64**LC** Eastleigh MR loco.

Boiler
No.1792 from new

Tender
BR1B No.1455 from new

Sheds
York 20/4/57
Scarborough 25/1/59
Normanton 14/6/59
Leeds Holbeck 16/6/63
Feltham 8/9/63
Shrewsbury 15/8/64

Withdrawn 7/8/65

One of the many BR Class 5s that found itself doing a spell here, at Shrewsbury shed; 73167 (with 41207 alongside) on 4 July 1965, weeks before withdrawal. AWS fitted. Another example of running without dome cover. Hamish Stevenson.

73168

To traffic 13/4/57

Works
4/57	E/DN/L/76 UK cast iron piston rod packing
20/9/57-30/9/57 **NC**	Doncaster
13/4/59-15/5/59 **HI**	Doncaster
	4983 ATC equipment
14/8/62-5/9/62 **HI**	Derby
7/1/64-25/1/64 **LC**	177,811 Eastleigh
	Overflow pipes and clips
17/9/64-14/10/64 **LC**	Eastleigh MR loco.

Boiler
No.1792 from new

Tender
BR1B no.1455 from new

Sheds
York 20/4/57
Scarborough 25/1/59
Normanton 14/6/59
Leeds Holbeck 16/6/63
Feltham 8/9/63
Shrewsbury 15/8/64

Withdrawn 7/8/65

73168 at Corkerhill on 7 January 1962; AWS battery box slung under cab. It was a Leeds Neville Hill engine at the time. All but one or two of the York ten went to the far south in their last years; in the case of 73168 its new home was Feltham. Hamish Stevenson.

73169

To traffic 26/4/57

Works
4/57	EDNL/76 Piston rod packing
17/12/59-28/1/60**HC**	Doncaster
26/2/60-12/3/60**LC**	Doncaster
13/5/61-19/5/61**NC**	Doncaster
28/8/61-30/9/61**LC**	Doncaster
	E/DN/L/76 UK cast iron piston rod packing
4/12/63-11/1/64**LI**	210,837 Eastleigh
7/4/64-25/4/64**NC-LC**	Eastleigh

Letter attached to weekly return, dated 4/5/64, from CMEE Department Brighton to Eastleigh Works Manager: *Referring to the letter dated 30th April from the Locomotive Manager, Castlefields House, agreeing to the repairs to Engine No.73169 being considered as a Return. I have made the new amendments to form BR9637 and BR9214 for the week ending 25/4/64.For C A Shepherd M and E Eng [General]*

Boiler
No.1794 from new

Tender
BR1B no.1457 from new

Sheds
York 26/4/57
Leeds Holbeck 5/5/57
Scarborough 25/1/59
Leeds Holbeck 20/6/59
Neville Hill 17/6/61
Wakefield 22/6/63
Feltham 16/9/63
Eastleigh 20/11/64

Withdrawn 10/66

73170

To traffic 17/5/57

Works
5/57	E/DN/L/86 Clearance on firebox support brackets [no date]
5/57	E/DN/L/76 UK cast iron piston rod packing
25/8/59-6/10/59**HI**	Doncaster. 4983 ATC equipment
21/9/61-27/10/61**GO**	Doncaster
5/12/63-18/1/64**LI-HI**	56,611 Eastleigh Overflow pipes and clips modified
31/12/64-25/1/65**LC**	Eastleigh

Boilers
No.1795 from new
No.1796 27/10/61

Tender
BR1B no.1458 from new

Sheds
York 18/5/57
Scarborough 25/1/59
Leeds Holbeck 14/6/59
Royston 9/9/62
Feltham 16/9/63
Eastleigh 20/11/64

Withdrawn 6/66

Finally we are at Nine Elms, 10 September 1966 with the highest numbered but not the last built BR Class 5, 73171. 'The Standard 5 is Good' wrote 'Mac' way back in 1951 in the 'Scottish Region Magazine' and so it proved. He went on: *I have never before travelled on an engine fitted with roller bearings, at least to the extent which exists on the standard design, and I had ideas on the subject. Such an engine should run more smoothly, it should also maintain speed on the level when coasting. Our engine proved both of these contentions right. I was writing notes legibly (for me) standing on the footplate at over 60mph. When the engine was coasting on a comparatively level stretch, I clocked each ¼mile post for almost three minutes until the brake was applied for a 'slow' and there was practically no diminution of speed until the brake was applied. That gives some rough and ready indication of the riding capabilities of the new 5'.* Peter Groom.

73171

To traffic 24/5/57

Works
25/4/59-2/6/59**HI** — Doncaster
10/8/61-22/9/61**GO** — Doncaster E/DN/L/76 UK cast iron piston rod packing
18/12/63-25/1/64**LI-HI** — 57,181 Eastleigh Overflow pipes and clips
540 monel metal stays riveted over 540 nuts renewed
151 new small tubes 'Stewart and Lloyds'
64 studs rivets and seams repaired 2 fusible plugs
22/6/65-1/7/65**NC** — Eastleigh

Boilers
No.1796 from new
No.1008 22/9/61

Tender
BR1B no.1459 from new

Sheds
York 15/6/57
LeesdsHolbeck 15/9/57
Royston 9/9/62
Feltham 16/9/63
Eastleigh 20/11/64

Withdrawn 10/66